I HATE TO BE RUDE BUT ...

THE SIMON COWELL

BOOK OF NASTY COMMENTS

I HATE TO BE RUDE BUT ...
THE SIMON COWELL
BOOK OF NASTY COMMENTS

TONY COWELL

FOREWORD BY
MICHAEL WINNER

PREFACE BY
PETE WATERMAN

JOHN BLAKE

Published by John Blake Publishing Ltd,
3 Bramber Court, 2 Bramber Road,
London W14 9PB, England

www.blake.co.uk

First published in paperback in 2006

ISBN 978 1 84454 522 3

British Library Cataloguing-in-Publication Data:

A catalogue record for this book is available from the British Library.

Design by www.envydesign.co.uk
Illustrations by Mike Mosedale

Printed in the UK by CPI Bookmarque, Croydon, CR0 4TD

1 3 5 7 9 10 8 6 4 2

© Text copyright Tony Cowell

Papers used by John Blake Publishing are natural, recyclable
products made from wood grown in sustainable forests.
The manufacturing processes conform to the environmental
regulations of the country of origin.

Every attempt has been made to contact the relevant
copyright-holders, but some were unobtainable. We would
be grateful if the appropriate people could contact us.

To Emma – for her love and support

FOREWORD

WHEN I first met Simon a few years ago he was totally unknown. I suppose his mother knew who he was, but hardly anyone else did. Actually I know his mother knew who he was because she was with him. And a delightful lady, too. Within twelve months Simon had become famous and then mega-famous. I can say with total sincerity that fame has not changed Simon. He was a pain in the arse then and thus he is now. Alright, I said that for effect. It isn't true. He's extremely pleasant, kind, well meaning and generally well behaved. Except that he is incapable of turning up anywhere on time which drives me bonkers.

Simon has taken a place in the nation's heart because he speaks without fear. He says things others would like to say but don't have the courage to say. Not unlike me, really. Most people edit their remarks. They flim-flam about. Simon is in the long line of supposedly rude TV talk-show people. I remember a gruff old sod called Gilbert Harding in the 50s. He spoke his mind and everyone got very irate about it. But they loved him as they do Simon. The other thing that's so good about Simon is that he has no pretension. He admits joyously to be interested in making money and not creating great art in the music world. Since recording artistes usually talk the most unbelievable crap about how important their work is and what it means in society, it's nice that a top executive believes in giving the public what they want regardless of phoney trimmings.

Simon has another rare quality. He's very generous. He always pays his way. And believe me that's rare in show business where there are more mean, tight, rich bastards than anywhere else. The only thing I could say that annoys me about Simon – apart from his perpetual lateness – is that when he's on the beach with me in Barbados (a) he wears black leather boots – which is very odd on the sand – and (b) his sunlounger is always surrounded by hordes of fans who he gives enormous time to. It's rather like sunbathing next to a bus stop. I've made a mental note to have him moved a bit further away next year. Other than that Simon is a breath of fresh air in our TV world of hypocrites and smarmies. And I think it's very clever that he's done so well when, if you put a time and motion study on how long he's on each TV show, it's a very small time for an enormous amount of money. Nothing wrong in that at all. Means you're likely to be around longer if you don't over expose yourself.

Yes, he's a nice fellow. I wish him continued luck. As a sign of my immense goodwill toward him I'm writing this foreword for no fee at all. Actually I forgot to ask for one and it's a bit late now. Still, I know Simon will give me one of his many Rolls Royce Phantom cars as recompense. Which is extremely nice of him. I'd like it in dark blue, please Simon, with grey leather upholstery. I only live round the corner so you won't have to spend too much on petrol getting it to me. Failing that a cheque for £50,000 wouldn't go amiss.

Michael Winner

PREFACE

THERE is a moment in everyone's life — it's that '*What?*' moment — when somebody says something so shocking you can't quite believe what you've just heard. Well, hearing Simon Cowell described as 'the pantomime baddie of British television' was my '*What?*' moment. It cast Neil Fox and me as Widow Twanky and Baron Hardup, with Nicky Chapman as Aladdin!

Looking back and thinking more seriously about it, it could be said that Simon has truly become that pantomime villain, and like all pantomime villains, yes, he is behind you and, yes, we all love to hate him! There's something incredibly satisfying in knowing that you can actually dislike Simon and he won't take offence!

Many of Simon's greatest quotes actually come from moments of boredom. And believe me he gets bored very easily! 'Oh no he doesn't!' Oh yes he does! I've known him not only in business but also as a friend for longer than it takes to rub a lamp and get a genie to appear. I have to say that at no point have we ever really fallen out. True, he has said some pretty daft things over the twenty-five years we've worked together, dropping me in it more times than anybody else in my life, not just on national television but at some pretty classic business meetings too. Like all great pantomime villains, he has a charming side that – at the end of the day – you just can't help but love! He can be, and often is, very generous with his comments and his deeds. In fact I could fill a book or maybe write a panto full of Simonisms, but then they beat me to it!

In truth, when we first started doing television together we hadn't a clue what we were doing. It didn't take long to learn, however, that it wouldn't work unless we acted naturally. The idea of working together as a team on television had come from a meeting at Celador. Simon and I were involved with the original series of *Who Wants To Be A Millionaire* when, after a classic Cowell-Waterman meeting, the guy from Celador turned around and said that we should have our own TV series as we were the best married couple they'd ever seen! He obviously didn't realise that he was watching a pantomime!

Simon's most difficult quality to live with is his wind-ups! Lucky for me (apart from once) I've never bitten and even when he gave out my mobile phone number on national television – typical Simon got the wrong one!

The success of *American Idol* is without a doubt down to Simon. I don't think any of us could have believed that it would have worked in the way that it did and that is truly thanks to Simon. The Americans obviously love pantomime villains just as much (if not more) than we do!

I always remember being told at school, 'If you're going to do it, do it well' and two things that Simon does well is sharp wit and cutting-edge comments. I'm stopped everywhere I go and it's always the same question: 'Is he really like that?' Yes, he really is and what you see is what you get!

I've never known Simon to be any different in all the time I've known him, so read the book and hiss and boo in all the right places, but remember that you'll be standing at the end and applauding!

Pete Waterman

ACKNOWLEDGEMENTS

I WOULD like to extend a huge personal thank you to all those who helped in the preparation of this book. I am very grateful to Michael Winner, Pete Waterman, Juliet at the Simon Cowell University, Jackie Lynn at the *Simon Times*, everyone at www.urdumped.com, Nikki Watkins at Sony BMG, Luke (thank God you backed up the files!), Eileen, my mother Julie, Malcolm and Penny Christopher, Nicholas and Katie for putting up with my monologues, Steve and Beverley at The Killigrew Inn Falmouth, everyone at Dermalogica, Mr Chow, Catherine

Memmi, Chaz Dean and the Hollywood Hair Guy. Thanks to Max Clifford for being there. A special thank you to Louis Walsh and Robson Green for not returning my calls. And of course thank you to my brother Simon for providing a small amount of amusing material.

CONTENTS

INTRODUCTION

'Nothing I say is premeditated. I've always been brittle.'
Simon Cowell

IN America, Simon Cowell is routinely
described as being 'bitchy', 'bullish', 'caustic',
'cruel', 'smug', 'arrogant' and 'brutally honest'.
In other words, they love him.

Less than three years ago, he was one of the
most hated people in the world. Even the
Queen was heard to remark, 'That dreadful
man' – and she wasn't referring to the Duke
of Edinburgh.

In the beginning, it was clear that nobody
actually got what Simon was all about. It

wasn't until the screening of the second series of ITV's *Pop Idol* and the birth of *American Idol* that the public, and Simon's critics, began to think that maybe he was telling the truth – or, as Simon would have it, 'People began to change their opinion of me because I tended to say what others only think.'

Let's face it: everybody is rude at some point or other, but it's how and why they're rude that counts. Anyone can scream and shout, but it takes class to be rude at the right time. It also helps if you're able to deliver a put-down in a humorous manner.

Simon achieves this effortlessly. A natural wit who thinks on his feet, he never reads from a script or an autocue and refuses to have anybody write or influence what he says to a contestant on any of the shows on which he appears. Bored rigid by the traditional after-dinner joke, he is the undisputed king of the sarcastic one-liner. Nobody does it better.

In the early days of *Pop Idol*, he was accused of 'turning the hopes and dreams of pop hopefuls into mincemeat'. 'He's too harsh, too rude, too nasty,' accused his critics. Nonsense. Over ten million viewers couldn't wait to tune into the show every Saturday night, and for one simple reason: to hear Simon tell wannabe pop stars the unvarnished truth: they just couldn't sing.

'If I said to most of the people who auditioned for these shows, "Good job, awesome, well done," it would have made me actually look and feel ridiculous. It's quite obvious most of the people who turned up for auditions were hopeless.'

Simon is original; there has never been anyone quite like him on television before. While he has since spawned a host of wannabe 'Mr Nasty' judges, there will only ever be one Simon Cowell – thank God! Simon *is* bitchy, bullish, caustic, cruel, smug, arrogant and brutally honest. He admits it. What he *is not* is a liar or a fake; what you see is what he is like in real life: a charming, funny, honest man with an ego the size of a planet.

THE LANGUAGE OF RUDENESS

Simon's honesty is his one redeeming quality that saves him from being just another pantomime grouch on a TV talent show. Indeed, he consistently begins his sentences in television and press interviews with 'If I'm being honest…'

This is a key phrase, normally the precursor to a cutting remark or a moment of rudeness. Indeed, it is central to his language of rudeness. What enables Simon to get away with being rude is his use of language. He makes rudeness funny; he employs an intelligent choice of words that form many a clipped, clean sentence that becomes a *death* sentence to many a pop-star wannabe.

The words Simon uses to form these death sentences are designed to create maximum impact. He frequently uses words such as 'appalling', 'terrible', 'dreadful', 'horrendous', 'hideous', 'ghastly' and 'abysmal' either on their own or as part of a sentence. Simon's cutting and intelligent sense of humour help blend these words into hard-hitting, cutting remarks that deliver a deadly message.

'There was one great part of your ghastly performance, and that was the end.'

'If this competition was all about looks, Pete Waterman wouldn't have made it on TV as a judge.'

'Terrible! Abysmal! You have the charisma of a wax dummy.'

Off the screen, Simon will use the same blend of sarcasm and wit when talking to the media about himself or other celebrities, often alongside a characteristic streak of self-deprecation:

'I have a confession to make: I dreamed about Paula [Abdul] last night. I think I woke up screaming.'

'I think that when people see me or read about me, they just think, "Bigmouth." I did this documentary [*Being Simon Cowell*] because people will only have seen me on *Pop Idol* and *American Idol*, and I thought it would be nice to show something else of my life. I hope it shows a very different side of me. I would say that I have a good sense of humour and can make light of a situation. I am not up my own arse, I am not too precious.'

'Daniel Bedingfield has recorded one of my favourite songs. The problem is that his ego is out of control. I may be allergic to him – I find him grotesque. My ego is a ping-pong ball compared to his moon.'

'I'm getting hundreds of emails every week and I have been threatened by people wielding baseball bats. People want to kill me — I just can't imagine why.'

Love him or loathe him, you have to admire Simon for being rude, honest and hysterically funny — and for changing the face of Saturday-night television.

Overall, though, I believe he is loved rather than loathed. So many people on TV are phoney. Simon Cowell says what everyone else is thinking. He's given a much-needed dose of reality to reality television. Real cruelty, after all, is letting people believe in a dream they can never live up to.

They say that fame changes people, but I can honestly say that Simon hasn't changed one bit. He always thought he was famous.

Tony Cowell,
November 2005

'I am not going to lie to these people
just because it makes them feel good.'

PART ONE

THE BIRTH OF THE BAD ONE

'Bad news, I'm afraid. Your voice is rubbish!'

THE EARLY YEARS

'From an early age I was very, very bad.'
Simon Cowell

START AS YOU MEAN TO GO ON

By the time Simon was four years old, he was already a fully grown rude boy. He refused to be disciplined, he had an opinion on everything and he never did as he was told. In the words of his mother, 'He was an horrendous child, worse than all my other sons.' Simon constantly insulted his parents, his brothers and anyone who had the guts to knock on the front door. He managed to make life at home a living hell. It was like growing up on the set of *The Omen*.

Everything had to revolve around him. He set the loft on fire, cut off his younger brother's hair, built his own pub in the garden shed and steadfastly refused to go to school. Even mealtimes became a nightmare for the family; he hated his mother's cooking, preferring instead a bizarre cocktail of Instant Whip, biscuits, ice cream, roast potatoes and toast – often all on the same plate.

Even today, Simon's interest in food is plain and childlike, his fridges in LA and London containing vast stocks of fish fingers, baked beans and spaghetti hoops, and posh eating remains a pet hate. 'I can't stand people who patronise you in restaurants because you don't order the right things,' he once said. 'It doesn't matter if you prefer baked beans to caviar. Who gives a shit? It you're paying for something, you're entitled to enjoy whatever you want. I would rather be happy eating my bowl of chips than pretend to enjoy a boiled pigeon with lobster sauce.'

4

THE EARLY NASTIES: RUDE BOY

Aged four: When asked whether he liked his mum's new fur hat, Simon replied, 'Mum, you look like a poodle.'

Aged five: To his music teacher during a lesson: 'Miss, this noise is dreadful. Why are you making us do it?'

Aged five: On meeting Liz Taylor, who lived next door, 'At that age, you take it for granted; it's just the neighbours. It was like, "Who's the girl with the big tits and all the diamonds?"'

Aged six: To actor Trevor Howard at a family party: 'I don't like actors.'

Aged seven: To his younger brother Nicholas: 'Father Christmas isn't real, and the quicker you come to terms with it, the better.'

Aged twelve: In his first letter to his parents from boarding school: 'Dear Mum and Dad. I hope you are finally glad to get rid of me and you are happy in your centrally heated house because I'm in a freezing cold dormitory with nothing to eat.'

Aged thirteen: In a letter to his parents from school: 'I have a sneaking suspicion that Newton's theory isn't going to play a huge part in my future.'

'I loved making money almost right from the start. From the age of seven, I was washing cars and mowing lawns. I got a real buzz out of being given cash for doing something.'

'I knew I wanted to be successful; I just didn't know how. I hated my boarding school, Dover College in Kent. I found it odd that I had to take subjects like geography or physics when they were never going to play any part in my future. I could speak English: what else was there to know?'

'I was never academically bright, but I was taught manners and the difference between right and wrong. I knew how far I could push things and get away with it, hopefully. My mum, Julie, taught me to always see the positive side of any situation. Dad taught me self-reliance.'

You have the charisma of a wax dummy.

THE SCHOOL OF HARD KNOCKS

'I was thick at school, there's no question. Thick and lazy. But I was ambitious. I only ever wanted to earn money.'

'FROM the age of eleven or twelve, I understood that most of the stuff I would be forced to learn would have no bearing on my future life. I don't know: woodwork, metalwork, physics and chemistry – what was the point?'

★

'I left school at sixteen with two O levels in English literature and language and spent another year doing retakes and got O-level sociology. But what with smoking and

9

drinking, I needed extra cash, so I worked as a waiter in a restaurant in Windsor. It was terrible – I caught a chef doing something unspeakable with a turkey once – but I was good and earned tips for being enthusiastic and fast.'

'When I was about twelve, we'd got onto a bus and, as a joke, pointed pea guns, which were plastic guns that shot dried peas. They'd go about five feet, the peas, but the guns looked like real guns and we pointed the gun at the driver and told him that we were hijacking the bus, and he actually believed us, so he didn't stop for about ten miles. And when we got to the other side, the police were waiting for us.'

'Why don't they have a lesson in school called Life, which teaches you about tax, the National Health Service, National Insurance, mortgages – all the things you actually need? Instead, they teach you how to burn chemicals.'

'I rebelled against school by failing everything. I'm not sure if I was thick or just bored, probably a combination of the two.'

'As a kid, I was horrendous: lippy, always getting a clip around the ear for being a smartass, which is one of the reasons I was reluctant to go on TV in the first place. I thought, "I am going to get into so much trouble. Forget it!"'

★

On first meeting a record company A&R man: 'I've never met such arrogant tossers. As far as I was concerned, they were idiots. I had a huge row with one guy. Halfway through playing my song, he took his boots and socks off and put his feet on the table. I told him to take his feet off his own desk. He refused and we ended up yelling at each other.'

'On a Sunday evening, the music to a religious programme would come on,

11

signifying the awful moment when the weekend was officially over. From then on, the countdown to school started. I used to feel sick to my stomach.'

On being reprimanded for wearing jeans at a job interview for supermarket Tesco: 'As a matter of fact, I don't really want to end up as a fifty-year-old bore sitting in an office the size of a telephone box, wearing a cheap suit. So I don't want the job, thanks.'

On his first job, working for an estate agent: 'My boss was a snotty, unhappy man. He hated me and I hated him.'

On working in the post room at record company EMI: 'People would try to make me feel inferior, laughing at me because I was delivering the post and they had better jobs than me. I dealt with it by ignoring them. I never let it get to me. I always thought the best way to deal with people like that was to do better than them, long-term. So, in a way, it made me more determined.'

'My father never really drummed too much into us – it was always left to my mother – but he used to say that, when you work for a company, you have to look after yourself first.'

On losing his father in 1999: 'Nothing ever prepares you for losing your father, and part of me believed it would never happen. I had to fly back to London to get home to Mum, and I was glad I had fourteen hours on the plane. When something bad happens, I'm like an animal: I need to retreat.'

'I was very popular at school because I was the one with the big mouth who was always in trouble.'

'You sang like someone who sings on a cruise ship.
Halfway through, I imagined the ship sinking.'

WE ARE FAMILY . . .

'Simon will date any woman, as long as there's a
pole in front of her.'
Nicholas Cowell, Simon's younger brother

'He was always a weedy kid and a bit lippy,
and still is, but Simon is brilliant at what he
does. He just goes out there and says exactly
what he thinks. It's not an act, and all of this
hasn't changed him. What you see is what
you get. He's the same person he's always
been: sarcastic, funny and very sharp. But
he's got dreadful taste in music. The last
time I was at his house, he had one of those
CD players where you can stick two

hundred CDs in, and he only had three in there: Frank Sinatra, Robson and Jerome, and *Summer Hits of 1983.'* – *Nicholas Cowell*

'It's much better that you end up with a lot of money in your bank account rather than a gold clock after fifty years' service.' – *Eric Cowell, Simon's late father*

'Simon has a twinkling air of mystery. He's able to look at you in a way where it's impossible to know what he's thinking or, more importantly, what he's going to say. Genius!' – *Luke Cowell, Simon's nephew*

'On the morning of my wedding, I was staying with Simon's parents, having breakfast in bed, when suddenly Simon [aged six] barged into the room, dived down the bed and out the other side, shouting, "When I go to bed, I wear pyjamas. Why don't you?"' – *Penny Christopher, Simon's cousin*

'I think of Simon as a naughty schoolboy, sniggering at the back of the class. He just loves making trouble; it's what he lives for – apart from money! He just loves stirring up trouble, but he's not vindictive. I'm just glad I married his brother. For me, the funniest day is having Sunday lunch at his mum's and watching Simon, Nicholas and Tony together. It's ten times funnier than anything on *The X Factor*.' – *Katie Cowell, Simon's sister-in-law*

★

'Understand one thing in life, son. Every single person who works for you has an invisible sign on their forehead saying, "Please make me feel important."' – *Eric Cowell*

MUM'S THE WORD

'I've never known him to be rude to anyone. He was brought up to think good manners were important.'

17

'Simon's a great son but, like anyone else, he needs putting into line sometimes. I won't stand for some of the things he says on television. To me, he's still my little boy, and he's very nice. Really! If there are any nice girls in America who want a husband, he's free. After he said "bollocks" on *Pop Idol*, I said to him, "Simon, you're forty-four years old and you *do not* swear on national television."'

'As a child, he was horrendous, worse than all my [other] boys. Simon's youngest brother, Nicholas, had piano lessons, so Simon had to have guitar lessons. They competed with each other at everything – football, girls – and they're still competing now, only these days it's about who's got the best car.'

'Simon was hopeless at school and didn't impress his teachers. There were no signs he was going to be a big talent at all. Today, I don't see him as "Mr Nasty"; he's a caring person, always the first to help anybody. Of course he's tough – you need to be in showbusiness – but he also has a very sensitive side, and at first he found the cruel comments being written about him as difficult to take as I did.'

'I hated it when Simon started going to lap-dancing clubs and I told him I didn't like him mixing with girls like that. Naturally, he didn't take a blind bit of notice.'

'By the way, he's got a dreadful voice and he can't dance.'

'I despair. At school we drum into them that there's no such thing as failure... then they meet Simon Cowell!'

TV: THE BIRTH OF THE X-TERMINATOR

'I am poor, misunderstood Simon. [Actually,] I'm really the
nice one, and no one gets it yet, but they soon will.'
Simon Cowell

In January 2000, Simon arrived back from
holiday in Barbados, tanned but very bored.
The success of Robson and Jerome had
already made him a millionaire, and he was
then riding high on the success of his band
Westlife. What he yearned for was to find new
ways of selling more records and making
more money. Nothing new there, then.

Television was to provide the answer.
Reality television first hit the UK that same
summer, with *Big Brother* and *Survivor* going

head to head in the ratings. But it was a new music talent show named *Popstars* that was to give Simon a rather bright idea:

'*Popstars* was brilliant TV, but it lacked something: me!'

'I realised very early on the impact of TV on record sales. I pioneered children's TV record spin-offs with *Zig & Zag* and *The* [Mighty Morphin] *Power Rangers*. I offered the BBC £500,000 for the Teletubbies' single and I'd never even seen the show. People used to laugh and say, "You're selling records with *wrestlers?*", and I thought, "Yes, for the moment." By the time *Pop Idol* aired – the first time I went on TV – I was forty-one, and I'd seen how sudden publicity can turn people into jerks, so I knew the pitfalls and accepted it for what it was. When it all began, I had to be dragged kicking and screaming in front of the cameras. So the idea that I love it, that I play up to it, is absurd. I wasn't particularly interested in being on

television. I never really went into this – unlike a lot of people who judge these shows – to be a personality *per se*.'

★

On *Popstars: The Rivals*: 'I only saw one show and just watched in horror as I saw this blind kid not knowing what way he was walking and this girl about to go into labour. I looked at the panel and thought, "What on earth are you doing?"'

★

On judge Nigel Lythgoe's dress sense: 'He must have been sponsored by C&A, who closed down shortly afterwards, of course.'

★

'It's easy to be an asshole on TV, but after a while people could see I wasn't trying to be rude. I was actually truthful in what I was saying. As long as you're saying what people are thinking, you're no longer an idiot.'

★

'The one motivation that makes anyone go onto TV for a talent competition, or even

Survivor, is very simply either a desire for fame or a desire for money. And if you haven't got the mentality to cope with that, then simply don't enter the competition.'

POP IDOL — MR NASTY OR MR POPULAR?

'What made *Pop Idol* funny was when someone was horrendous but was not aware that they were horrendous. We had a lot of people like that who had absolutely no idea how bad they were.'

Simon Cowell

'The most important thing *Pop Idol* has done for me is that, for the first time in my life, I feel I'm almost in control of my destiny. Before *Pop Idol*, I'd go away at Christmas and think, "What am I going to do next year, apart from get bored?"'

★

'Pete Waterman was put on the show simply because I thought it'd be good TV, and he's very opinionated, which takes the heat off me. He is the one person in the world who's got a bigger mouth than me and is fundamentally more unpleasant. He's wittier than me, he's genuinely funny – I think I just come across as a bit miserable, a bit fed up.'

'The public may not agree with me, but I'm not going to sell myself short just to be Mr Popular. We have been consistently critical throughout these TV shows and I'm not about to change.'

ON THE FINALISTS OF THE FIRST SERIES

'Some people say that Korben's problem was that he was flamboyantly gay.'

'Jessica Garlick was in awe of Pete Waterman to the point where it was like watching a pathetic schoolgirl with a horrible crush. Pete loved it, of course.'

'Aaron Bailey was a nice bloke with a nice voice, who drove a train. One minute he was driving the 8:30 from London to Crewe, and suddenly he's singing to millions of people on national television.'

'Laura Doherty spent the longest time in make-up and appeared to have the thinnest skin. She also began to believe in her own hype.'

'Rosie Ribbons sang "The Winner Takes It All", which is probably why she didn't.'

'Hayley Evetts was good-looking but had no chance of having a hit record.'

'Zoe Birkett turned into a performing doll. Nobody would sign her.'

'Darius Danesh had so much charm that, when he met my mum, she started acting like a twenty-year-old. His ambition outweighs

his talent. I'll be open with Darius: he is one of the most charismatic people I've ever met, but he should be running a cult.'

★

'When Gareth Gates hit the headlines for shagging Jordan, I thought, "So what? He's eighteen and she's a pin-up." If she comes on to you, you're going to shag her – I would have – although the pregnancy thing kind of puts you off.'

★

'I never hit it off with Will Young. I blame myself for not being able to work with him. I lashed out, which was the wrong thing to do. I don't think he'd want to work with me in a million years, which is a shame because I rate him as an artist. Will is a better singer than Gareth [Gates] – there's no doubt about that in my mind – but Gareth was the pop idol. And at the end of the day, both of them have done bloody well.'

SIMON SAYS

'My attitude is, if you think it, say it.'

To Leon McPherson: 'You sounded like a warped record.'

'Your problem, Natalie, was you chose a stage song and you're not good enough to be on stage, let alone [being] a pop idol.'

To Warren Wald: 'I don't think anyone in London is as bad as you, and London is a big city. Off you go, goodbye!'

To Lisa after she sang 'The Power of Love': 'That song does one of two things: it either transfixes you because it is a beautiful song or it sends you to sleep. And you fell into the latter – we've had the musical version of Valium.'

To Daniel Webster: 'You're one of the worst singers I've heard in my life. You were diabolical, crap!'

To Heather: 'Your voice isn't even good enough for a cruise ship.'

To Nicola Thomas: 'Butlin's, yes. *Pop Idol*, no.'

★

To forty-two-year-old Brendan Killkenny: 'You're not going through to the next round. A, because you can't sing, and B, because you're over twenty-six. So why are we bothering having this conversation? Goodbye! There's no point, there's nothing else to say. Goodbye!'

On Darius Danesh's performance of 'Let's Face the Music and Dance': 'He sounded like some ghastly singer in a hotel lobby. If I'd had a tomato in my pocket, I would have thrown it at him!'

'Rick Waller just became a sore loser. It was only because of the show that he got the publicity, and then he just turned on us, so it was total good riddance.'

After Simon said 'Bollocks' to Pete Waterman on the show: 'I don't apologise for swearing on live TV, it just popped out. But there wasn't a better word in the English dictionary to sum out what came of Pete Waterman's mouth. "Bollocks" was just perfect.'

'The object of this competition is not to be mean to the losers but to find a winner.'

'My act is going to run out really quickly I have no inclination to be doing this in five or ten years' time.'

'I've never ever rehearsed a line or written down anything that I say on the show because then you turn it from a reality show into a pantomime and the public know.'

'I think we are entitled to stop boring people entering these competitions because boring people don't sell records.'

'I really can't see myself doing this for much longer because, to be truthful, the public will get bored of me.'

To Carla Winters: 'You are not Manchester United: you are Dagenham.'

'If I tell someone they have a terrible voice, it's a kindness. Some of them honestly believe they're Madonna or Lionel Ritchie, and it's bloody obvious that they're not.'

'We've had some fun with *Pop Idol*, but what it really comes down to is this: that in England and America, for quite a while now, we have been told by the powers that be about political correctness. You can't say this; you can't say that. That's a little bit like saying, "You're not allowed to speak your mind in public any more."'

'We live in a fame epidemic — it's like a disease — and ninety-nine per cent of the people who turn up are useless. They're just not aware of it. And that's the disease.'

'People have said I'm vain. I don't think I am, actually. I took a lot of stick over what I wore on *Pop Idol*, and I thought it was hysterical — really, really funny.'

To Will Young after the singer's rendition of 'Light my Fire': 'I had a vision of Sunday lunch, and after Sunday lunch you say to your family, "I'm now going to sing a song for you." Distinctly average, I'm afraid. I just thought it was totally normal, in the context of the show. I honestly didn't think it was good enough.'

Will Young's response: 'I think it's nice that you have given opinions on this show. I think that, in previous shows, you haven't; you've just given projected insults, and it's been terrible to watch. I think that on this show you've been better, and I think you've given opinions and you've backed up your opinions. It *is* your opinion, but I don't agree with it. I don't think it was average – I don't think you could ever call that average. But it is your opinion, and I respect that, so thank you very much.'

★

Oops!

THE X FACTOR: SERIES ONE, 2004

'There isn't a nice way of telling people
they haven't got any talent.'
Simon Cowell

ON SHARON OSBOURNE

'Sharon has not worked in the music
business for years and, let's face it, she hasn't
done the best job in the world of managing
her daughter.'

'If Sharon were a dog, she would be one of
those over-bred Pomeranians, fluffy and
feisty, whereas Louis is a kind of mutt dog
with big, appealing eyes that knows how to

get things. I'm more of a cat because I don't like being stroked.'

'First [Sharon] says I rig *The X Factor*, then I don't know talent, then I chase all the young girls. Now I'm gay. If a flood wipes out Britain next week, she'll blame me for that as well.'

'Sharon's like one of those fish at the bottom of the ocean that don't do anything till you swim near them, and then they bite you from nowhere.'

ON LOUIS WALSH

'Louis is in a world of his own. He still thinks the Eurovision song contest is great and that nobody over twenty-three should be a pop star. He's stuck in a time warp. He's like Sharon's lap dog, a replacement for the yappy things she has at home.'

ON THE SHOW

'I'd say ninety per cent of the people who turned up [on *The X Factor*] were awful. We had everything from an eighty-one-year-old granny to a sixty-five-year-old woman trying to pass herself off as a twenty-year-old. A lot of them got a dose of reality; there were more tears and tantrums on this show than I've ever seen in my life.'

'Where there's a hit, there's a writ. I had five writs when I launched *The X Factor*.'

'The biggest moaners [on *The X Factor*] are always the fat people.'

When asked who he thought liked Steve Brookstein: 'David Bowie, Mick Jagger, Prince Philip phoned me last Tuesday, the Pope has sent me an email. We've got a lot of celebrity support, but we don't like to boast about it.'

'I know when someone walks into audition, even before they've sang, if they're going to be terrible. In a real-life audition, as they walk in, I would just say, "Do a U-turn, don't even bother singing."'

ON BEING SIMON COWELL

'I believe that all I'm doing is saying what most people are thinking. So, if that's being a bastard, I don't think I am. For the first time, we're showing people what the music business is really like; it's tough.'

'I think most people I know have rude thoughts; they think mean things. I'm much more comfortable with somebody telling me to my face the way they feel about me and I'm much more comfortable doing the same thing in return.'

'I've been popular on these shows because I've had the guts to say what other people would normally want to say but haven't said for fear of upsetting fat people, minorities or whatever. I hate being told what I can or cannot do.'

'What I try to do on the show is say what I would be saying at home. I think I'm like a public service, really.'

'What you must never do on a show like this is be gratuitous for the sake of being gratuitous. Otherwise you just turn into a caricature of yourself.'

'When you appear on TV, you do become more attractive to girls. Even Les Dennis can pull because he's on TV!'

SIMON SAYS
'I will take a £1 million bet that Matt

[Johnson] is not in the finals. He has a less than one per cent chance of getting through.'

ON THE CONTESTANTS

To Roberta Howett: 'Is this girl a star or someone who should be in a hotel?'

To forty-nine-year-old Verity: 'I see you in a garden pruning roses.'

To girl band Caution: 'You look like ice skaters who've been locked up for fifteen years.'

After Paul Holt sang 'End of My World': 'It's the end of your singing career, that's for sure.'

To a dance-star wannabe: '[Your performance was] like an audition for *One Flew Over the Cuckoo's Nest*.'

To camp Essex lad Darren: 'You look like Princess Diana.'

To Josh McGuire: 'If I was going to give you some career advice, I would say you should be more of a drag queen.'

To Ben David Wynne: 'You have as much credibility as a rapper as George Formby does.'

To Sarah Louise: 'You're proof that you can't sing and dance.'

To boy band G4: 'You all look like bankers.'

On Rowetta: 'She was amazing, but she is completely and utterly barking mad.'

To contestant Simon Cowl: 'I'm going to say something I've never wanted to say: "Simon Cowl, you were absolutely useless!"'

'Frankly, we'd have been better off if the night had stayed silent. Sorry, but this Christmas just isn't going to be merry.'

On Steve Brookstein: 'It's one thing getting a medal; it's another selling records.'

On voting Rowetta through to the next round: 'Occasionally, you make decisions you're going to regret.'

'Pop for me is old news, it's over. I think the public want something different, which is probably why Steve Brookstein won *The X Factor*.'

'Telling someone they have zero talent is actually a kindness.'

THE X FACTOR: SERIES TWO, 2005

'This year we have defined *The X Factor* as the
musical version of *Little Britain*.'
Simon Cowell

'It's important that this show doesn't become
about two middle-aged people having a
ridiculous argument, which is what it turned
into. It's got to be focused on the people who
enter the competition, otherwise it becomes a
sideshow for something stupid.'

When Sarah's world came to a shattering end
after the judges refused to send her through
to the next round, her tearful family fell to

their knees and begged Simon to reverse the decision. His response? 'I don't know whether it's the moment they're caught up in, or whether I'm being harsh or kind. Who's being worse: the family who are encouraging her to a achieve a dream she's never going to achieve or me, who just cuts it dead? I, personally, think I'm the kinder one.'

On voting off Maria: 'I made the wrong decision. If I'd have had five minutes more to think about it, I would have sent The Conway Sisters home. I acted out of loyalty, but this show is about talent. Maria should have stayed. The Conways don't have a chance of winning this competition.'

'I get bored of watching twenty-two-year-olds coming onto a talent show and saying, "Make me famous."'

'Of course, ninety per cent of the auditionees are completely nuts, but that's what this show is all about. Some performances are beyond scary, but I've seen a lot of people who really have something special.'

After Nicholas was voted off: 'Louis is an idiot. He has been tremendously stupid: he came into this competition bragging that he had the winner, that he had the show all sewn up, but with the wrong song choices and the wrong management Louis has managed to muck it all up.'

'People think that if you don't write your own material, you can't be taken seriously. Well, let them think that – what the fuck do I care?'

'If you read the papers, you'd think it was a matter of life or death but the truth is, it's a mad talent show. Can you imagine if a tape of the show were buried in a time capsule? When people dug it up and watched it, they'd think everyone in Britain in 2005 was afflicted by mass dementia.'

'It's clear that Sharon will do anything to win and to stop me winning, even if it means teaming up with Louis. I didn't realise how competitive they both would be. They have both taken everything extremely seriously, which I find bizarre. I don't really care, though: I'm confident I have the skills to win.'

'I met someone the other night after the show who's twenty-eight-years-old and he hasn't worked a day since he left college because he's pursuing a dream he'll never, ever realise. He thinks he's a great singer. Actually, he's crap, but nobody has said to him, "Why have you been wasting your time for eight years?"'

'At one point, *The X Factor* seemed a little bit like we'd only opened it to people from the loony bin or something.'

'There are occasions when you watch the auditions on TV and they say that their dog died that morning and that they hope, in memory of their dog, to get through. Then they sing, I tear them to pieces and they walk out and burst into tears. But I never feel guilty about it.'

'Today's youth have grown up with so much praise that they don't know how to deal with a little honesty. I'm just telling useless people who can't sing that they can't sing. I'm not drowning puppies here.'

'A friend told me I was a complete tosser last night on TV and when I watched it back I could see they were right. It's never pleasant, but it's normally correct. You just shake yourself down and try not to be a tosser again. A lot of people I know make a name projecting themselves as really nice family people who are cheating behind their girlfriends' backs. That is what I can't stand; I loathe that. At least everything I do is out there. I'm not perfect. I have a slight distrust

of people who go out of their way to be nice –
I wonder what they're hiding.'

Speaking on ITV's *This Morning* following
Louis Walsh's walkout: 'The real trouble is
finding someone bland enough to replace
Louis. Where do you start? It's hard being
stupid. It's definitely not as hard as it looks,
but Louis does it brilliantly.'

SIMON SAYS

To forty-seven-year-old twins Maura and
Sally, who sang a collection of ABBA songs:
'You're not ABBA: you're Flabba!'

On boy band The Brothers: 'They're more
current and interesting than just another boy
band. The only problem is, Louis would have
them wearing blazers within a week.'

To sheep farmer Justin White: 'I was expecting something a little more rugged. You sound like a three-year-old girl!'

To a gutted Tony: 'You're someone who will always be performing to people holding peanuts, ie in a bar. You do not have star quality.'

To Fiona Rae Griffiths: 'You look like Vicky Pollard, and your friend looks like a stretched version of her.'

To Trevor Hodgson: 'I'm absolutely gobsmacked – you could sell a lot of records.'

To Louis and Sharon after they had voted Chico through to Boot Camp: 'You're making a fool of yourselves and a fool of the competition.'

When voting off Chico on the series' first live show: 'I'm sending Chico home. And I'll pay for the flight.'

On Chico after he was finally voted off: 'He'll make loads of money and get a lot of girls. That will suit him fine.'

'We'll definitely have to have Louis back next year. It just wouldn't be the same without him. Besides, what else is he going to do? It's the best job in telly.'

'My ego has reached its peak. Its just that the others on the programme haven't.'

★

'The programme is a snapshot of this country: funny and sad in parts.'

AMERICAN IDOL:
THE RUDE AWAKENING

'I'm going to be doing the show in America next year and
I'm going to be the Joan Collins of pop TV.'
Simon Cowell, October 2001

'Simon Cowell is an asshole. That's what he's famous for: the needlessly brutal insults of the more hapless contestants on the fame-seeking spectacle *American Idol*. Even the series' own site says that Cowell "became a celebrity in his own right for reducing a string of teenage wannabes to tears while serving as a judge on the UK version of the show." Cowell represents the asshole as truth-teller' – Rob Walker, *Slate*

Simon on the first *American Idol* show: 'It's all gone a bit mad as far as I'm concerned, and I've got a return flight booked; I'm ready to leave if the wrong thing happens. I will be really, really upset if the right person doesn't win this competition. [The show's called] *American Idol*. It's not called "Boy with the Most Sympathetic Story Idol". It's about talent!'

'It's a show which is run by the public. In my opinion, it's the only fair competition on TV at the moment. Regardless of what I say or what Paula says, or what Randy says, the viewers decide who's going to stay or go. I'm not going to lie to these people just because it makes them feel good.'

'There are obviously people out there rebelling against all the insincerity. People in America want something more honest than the sugar-coated rubbish you get most of the time.'

'God forbid the show ever becomes predictable.'

'I would say America is almost becoming as good a judge as me.'

'You've got to always look at this show with one raised eyebrow. It's a fun show to do and you must never take it too seriously. We all know that the majority of the people who turn up on a show like this are completely disillusioned. This is a reality check.'

'As a judge, you always want it to work. But then, I'm a viewer, and as a viewer I want to see controversy because the minute we've lost the controversy, we've lost a hit show. That's why I always fight against sanitising the show. It's a reality show and you've got to allow for things to go wrong, and they will.'

'I can't stand all this pretend hugging. It's crap. These people should hate each other's guts. Why should they want another contestant to do well? They must be thinking, "I'd better hug him. The camera is on me." It's unbelievable to watch.'

'Every single person you see audition – every one – believes they are the best singer in America.'

On hosting the auditions for *American Idol*: 'I loathe it. It's like undergoing dental treatment without anaesthetic. But we've sold millions of records in the US on the back of this.'

'I'm not famous; I'm well-known. Is it better to be well known than not? In my job, yes, because it opens doors. I do get approached, but it's not a bad thing. It shows you that people like the show, and that's all I care about.'

'What we are saying to people is, "I'm sorry to disappoint you, but guess what? You actually need to have talent to be on this show."'

'Anyone who enters a competition like this is going to probably end up in two years' time with an entourage of fifty, isn't going to return any phone calls and is doing it for themselves. There's nothing wrong with that. That's why most people decide they want to become famous.'

'I think I'm the only sincere judge out of the three of us because I say what I feel to their faces.'

'I'm saying to all these people, "Don't waste your time." I'm actually the kind one because the Paula Abduls of this world would say, "You're fantastic. Take a few singing lessons and you'll become rich and famous overnight." Believe me, they won't.'

★

'The majority of people who turn up on the show are completely delusional. The thing about *American Idol* is that you can't cheat it and we haven't got a clue what's going to happen – it's a bit like the lions and the Christians.'

'It's great that in a very PC world we're allowed to run a show where we tell someone who's ugly, "You're ugly." Otherwise, it can be safe and boring, and I can't stand that. There's a lot of insincerity, people saying, "God sent me here." No, He didn't! You're here because you want to be rich and famous, like everyone else. This show is all about finding a star, not feeling sorry for people who aren't very good.'

'I don't ever feel bad about what I say to people on the show, and I'll tell you why: because ninety per cent of the people who turn up for our auditions have a false impression of their abilities. Somebody at some point in their lives has to tell them the truth. I'm like the friendly executioner. I think what I do is kinder than patronising somebody with false hope.'

'I never get tired of being a jerk. I'm English – we're all jerks. It's the way we've been brought up by our parents. We're very repressed, we're a strange country.'

'I am not going to lie to these people just because it makes them feel good.'

'I think I come over as a bit smug and self-righteous at times, and I imagine that could be annoying.'

'I'm not bothered about whether people are fat or thin. Provided that they've got charisma, they can be huge. Look at Pavarotti or Meat Loaf. You don't even think about their size; it's just them – great personalities, great voices, great aura. There is a difference, however, between being big and being out of shape.'

'My job is to try to say what the audience is thinking at home. What I've said from day one on *American Idol* is that it doesn't matter how many people turn up; only two are going to be any good. So why give everybody else false hope? Because it's such a tough business.'

'I couldn't care less what I say to anyone on the show. I think I'm more likely to jump off a bridge than to give them false hope [only for them to] find out in seven or eight years' time that they've wasted their life.'

'You can have your stomach stapled, and I'm going to have my mouth zipped. I swear it works before my brain. There isn't a week that goes by where at the end I'm not thinking, "Why did I do or say *that?*"'

'Some people say, "Yes, of course *American Idol* has a finite life, and all good things have to come to an end." But there's another argument that says maybe this is the musical Superbowl. Maybe it could run for twenty years.'

AMERICAN IDOL: JUDGING THE JUDGES

'Randy and Paula go out of their way to make me look good.'

Simon Cowell

ON PAULA ABDUL

'Paula, you should be the first female president of this country.'

★

'Paula, it sounds like you have a comedy writer. Please sue him.'

★

'I find it easier to get on with Paula. Sharon [Osbourne] gobs off to the press the whole time. I think that if you're going to say something to someone, you should say it to their face.'

'[Paula's] a diva. "Diva" means "successful, spoilt female artist", and she's a feisty little girl who wants her own way. She fancies me. In fact, I think she's in love with me. But I'm afraid the feelings are just not mutual.'

'I admire Paula for admiring me.'

'If Paula can't get her own way, she goes nuts. Normally at me.'

'Paula is a pain in the ass. She's just one of those irritating people. I agree with some of what she says, but I disagree with a hell of a lot of what she says. I keep my time with her to a minimum.'

'She likes me, she hates me – she can't have me!'

'I don't wish Paula any harm. I don't wish her bad luck. Will we be having dinner together in six months' time? Never! Maybe it's the fact that I'm on planet Earth and she's on planet Venus.'

'Normally, you can tell what somebody will be like, sexually, by her facial expressions. Paula's actually got a very naughty face. I think she is quite sexy.'

'My attitude is, if someone's going to criticise me, tell me to my face. I find Paula patronising. It's as simple as that. Paula is more damaging than I am to these contestants because a lot of people just shouldn't be singing for a living.'

ON RANDY JACKSON

'Who would want to pick a fight with Mount Kilimanjaro?'

On Randy's weight loss: 'Actually, he looks like someone let some air out. He was so big, and when you let the air out of those bouncy castles, it all kind of goes like that.'

'What I love about Randy Jackson is that I have never, ever seen this guy down. He is somebody who genuinely lights up a room. He has the best energy I've ever come across in my life.'

ON HOST RYAN SEACREST

'Did you see it? He wore a see-through blouse! The words "fashion" and "disaster" come to mind.'

'If you think you can find thirty-two great singers instead of two, you'll be a billionaire instead of a thousandaire.'

'I see Ryan crying quite a lot. It's probably to do with the fact that his hairdresser hasn't turned up on time or something.'

On Ryan being honoured on Hollywood's Walk of Fame: 'Other people doing well just naturally makes me unhappy. It's one of those things you dread.'

'We encourage mediocrity on this show. It's how Ryan Seacrest got the job.'

ON THE CONTESTANTS

'I'm not in this business to worry about people's feelings. I'm in this business to find the best possible talent, period.'

'I hope on the next show we get some good-looking people because I don't want the show to become known as "Ugly Idol".'

'Not everybody is perfect, and I don't think we should be looking for perfect people.'

SIMON SAYS
'You have to have a talent to progress it. I don't believe Cassandra has a singing talent. She's completely wasting her money. Sorry.'

On rocker contestant Constantine Maroulis: 'I found Constantine very amusing, and we do miss him. When I hear these people described as "rockers", it makes me laugh because rock 'n' roll, by definition, is anti-establishment, and you can't get more establishment than *American Idol*. I mean, the irony of it is hilarious.'

On *American Idol* winner Carrie Underwood: 'I think Carrie is reflective of what's going on in [the US]. There are a lot of girls saying, "I'm bored of girls dressing like sluts. I'm bored of regressive rap lyrics. I actually just like a clean-cut girl because I'm a clean-cut girl.' There's a difference between what the record industry thinks and what Wal-Mart customers think. That's one of the reasons why Carrie is doing so well.'

On Clay Aiken: 'I would never, ever in a million years have offered Clay Aiken a record contract if he'd walked into my office – and I would have been wrong. That's what makes the show exciting.'

'You sing like that and you will never, ever get through an audition. It was absolutely painful to listen to.'

On guest judge Kenny Loggins: 'The judging equivalent of Valium.'

On Justin Guarini: 'I think he was a very good wedding singer. He thought he was the new Usher. He was actually more Barry Manilow than Usher, but he didn't realise it.'

'I don't see the point of doing anything that makes you sound like a dog. That's why I hate yodelling.'

To Andrew Chester: 'You have wasted everyone's time. And it's not just a "no", it's a "never!"'

'I think you have to understand the difference between a dream and a nightmare. What we have just experienced was a nightmare.'

'I'm not being rude, but you can't sing. There is no pleasure to derive from your performance.'

'That was possibly the worst audition I have ever heard. Not only can you not sing; you have a very strange sound.'

'That sounded like Stevie Wonder with a really bad cold.'

'Have you ever seen the film *The Wedding Singer*? Because that's what you sound like.'

'I could only describe your voice as ghastly.'

'I think you are a boring performer.'

'You are gorgeous, but your voice isn't.'

'You had to pull out the performance of a lifetime to last another week. You didn't!'

'Terrible, abysmal. I would say, not a cat in hell's chance!'

'You sounded like a ship sinking.'

'If I had to choose one idol to go out to dinner with, it would be Fantasia Barrino. I like her.'

'If your lifeguard duties were as good as your singing, a lot of people would be drowning.'

'I think you are suffering from something called delusion.'

'Good isn't necessarily good enough. And I don't think that performance merits you being proclaimed American Idol. It's as simple as that.'

'If you were singing like this two thousand years ago, people would have stoned you.'

'You sing like Mickey Mouse on helium.'

'In a competition full of hamburgers, you are a steak.'

To Mikalah Gordon: 'Your confidence exceeds your ability.'

'You dress better than you sing, and you got dressed in the dark.'

To Scot Savol: 'I've been figuring out for

weeks why you're still in the competition. You are Ordinary Guy who is doing quite well. Ordinary Guys can get up at karaoke and entertain the audience.'

'Singing involves giving pleasure. You can't! You also look like you have been dragged through a bush.'

To Bo Bice: 'You may just have put thirty-four musicians out of work.'

To Anthony Fedorov: 'I think you need soul to sing that song. It's kind of like trying to have Woody Allen play the lead in *Shaft*.'

To Carrie Underwood: 'I have to discuss this look because it's like Barbie meets the Stepford Wives.'

To Carrie Underwood: 'That was the equivalent of you singing in the shower. You do it effortlessly.'

★

To Constantine Maroulis: 'I think the performance was akin to a waiter in a ghastly Spanish nightclub.'

To Vanessa Olivarez: 'You have a great personality, great voice, brilliant choice of song, but you have to lose a few pounds.'

To Patrick Fortson: 'I'm not being rude, but I think the outfit sucks. That is a terrible image.'

To Anthony Fedorov: 'It was pleasant, safe and a little insipid, so it's sort of a compliment.'

To Nadia Turner: 'That was the equivalent of musical wallpaper. When you're at a house, you notice the wallpaper but you don't remember it.'

To Carrie Underwood: 'It was a little like watching a kitten who wants to be a tiger.'

To Anwar Robinson: 'You've turned into the equivalent of a blanket: you're just sort of comforting and safe.'

To Carrie Underwood: 'It was rather like watching a washing-powder commercial in 1965.'

'I will give your vocal a seven, but I'm going to give your pouting a nine point five this week.'

'Honestly, based on that performance, if I were sitting in the karaoke bar, I'd be switching the microphone off.'

'You doing a sexy performance would be rather like Randy Jackson going on *Baywatch*.'

'Thank God it was only a one-minute song. We'd have had a full striptease after three minutes!'

To Bo Bice: 'A rocker doing *The Partridge Family*? It's rather like ordering a guard dog for your home and being delivered a poodle in a leather jacket.'

To Lindsey Cardinale: 'I think thirty million TV sets in America had their volumes turned down simultaneously tonight.'

To Janay Castine: 'Let me give you a horoscope: a suitcase and a plane ticket within twenty-four hours.'

To Mikalah Gordon: 'It looks like you've gone into an aging machine.'

'You're the musical equivalent of Ryan Seacrest.'

'You have as much Latin flair as a polar bear.'

'We could have been in a Portuguese nightclub in 1974.'

'It was like watching *The Exorcist*.'

★

'You had about as much passion as a kitten mewing.'

★

'You sang like someone who sings on a cruise ship. Halfway through, I imagined the ship sinking.'

★

'I think you're amazing: amazingly dreadful.'

★

'That was extraordinary. Unfortunately, extraordinarily bad.'

★

To semi-finalist Tenia Taylor, who tried to do her best Whitney Houston: 'It was an ambitious song for you to sing because I don't think you're that kind of singer. I don't think you're that good.'

★

'I can honestly say that you are the worst singer in America.'

'From one to ten, what would you give yourself? I'd give you a one. My advice would be, if you want to pursue a career in the music business, don't!'

To Cassandra, after Paula Abdul encouraged her to pursue a singing career: 'If you want to achieve what you want to achieve, you will not do it with your voice. Sorry.'

'Your audition was horrendous with a capital "H". What angers me is that people like yourself, who have the most attitude, have the least talent.'

To the weepy A.J. Gil, who went on to become a finalist: 'I think you're a boring performer. That laugh was hideous. I think you've blown it.'

'Are you taking singing lessons? Who's your teacher? Do you have a lawyer? Get a lawyer and sue her!'

'When you entered this competition, did you really believe that you could become an American Idol? [Contestant nods.] Well, then, you're deaf. Thank you, goodbye!'

To Jim Verraros: 'If you win this competition, we will have failed.'

'You looked like you were doing a Burger King commercial.'

On Nikki McKibbon, American Idol, 2002: 'As I watched her, I thought, "You are a better stripper than you are singer." I know that sounds rude, but that's what I felt.'

'Clay Aiken understood more than anyone else what made him popular and what people wanted to buy.'

★

'I remember Clay Aiken coming to see me eighteen months after the show, saying, "You were really rude about that red leather jacket." What? That was eighteen months ago, Clay.'

'It's kind of mystifying what happened to Fantasia. Maybe she didn't make the right record.'

To Scott Savol: 'Pack your suitcase tonight.'

To Vonzell Solomon: 'I have a horrible feeling that that wasn't as good as you thought it was. It was completely flat in the beginning.'

To Constantine Maroulis: 'It was a very bad imitation of the original.'

On Jim Verraros singing 'Easy': 'Jim was simply annoying because he was in the top ten and really didn't deserve to be. I remember sitting there, feeling miserable and thinking it was one of the most terrible things I had ever witnessed.'

★

On Clay Aiken singing 'Grease': 'If I had been watching this on TV, I would actually have run out of the room. This was a perfect example of how a performer can go from amazing to awful. The red leather outfit, the ghastly winks, the horrible hip dance. To say it was dreadful is an understatement.'

On Joshua Gracin singing 'Celebration': 'It was a musical nightmare. He had a cold that night, but I only wished it was laryngitis.'

To Jessica Sierra: 'You're a good singer, but you don't have the likeability factor.'

On Jim Verraros coming out: 'We were really shocked about that. I had no idea he was gay. Jim Verraros actually came up to me at a show and said, "Simon, I've got something to tell you." I said, "What?" He said, "I'm gay." I said, "Yeah?" He went, "Well, I've come out."

I said, "Jim, you came out the second you appeared on this bloody show!"'

ON AMERICAN IDOL FINALISTS, 2004/5

On Bo Bice and Constantine Maroulis: '"If I wore eyeliner and pouted, would I be more attractive?" I don't believe any of these guys are rock 'n' roll, and I'll tell you why: can you imagine the lead singer of Green Day singing "I Can't Smile Without You" with Carrie Underwood? I mean, give me a break.'

On Carrie Underwood: 'There's a movie called *The Mighty Wind*, and it's about a folk group reuniting. I looked at Bo and Carrie and I thought, "God, this is like a scene from that!"'

On Anthony Fedorov: 'He's a little angel. It's only when he does that Latin dancing that it's, "Oh, shut up, Anthony!"'

'I have a real problem with boredom. I also have a massive fear about not being in control of my own destiny. The great thing about this show is that, for the next two to three years, I have a way of controlling my own destiny.'

'You sing like Mickey Mouse – on helium.'

PART TWO

TURNING THE TABLES

CONTESTANTS HAVE THEIR SAY

'Loads of women fancy Simon. He is a sex symbol. He eyes women up and they go all weak at the knees. I do love him.'

Rowetta, *The X Factor*, **2004**

'You wouldn't know a superstar if it hit you on the nose.' – Chico, *The X Factor*, 2005

★

'Simon doesn't give a shit about anyone else as long as he gets attention.' – Kurt Nilsen, *World Idol* winner

★

'It seems *The X Factor* is not based on talent this year. It's based on the judges.' – Mike Hannides, *4Tune*

'The public no longer listen to what Simon Cowell thinks. Once his word might have been gospel, but not any more." – Mark Rhodes, *Pop Idol* runner-up

'I do believe that [Simon's] world is about to come crashing down around him very soon – at least, I hope so. I hate him. I'm surprised no one has ever punched Simon Cowell.' – Rik Waller

'I think Simon Cowell is an arrogant man who is more concerned with image than real talent. He only seems to want people with spiky hair who look like they've just walked out of Top Man.' Jesus, *The X Factor*, 2004

'Simon, I think with your waistband being so high, you might want to undo it one notch because it's restricting the blood flow to your head.' – Darius Danesh, *Pop Idol*, 2003

'I am hurt and I am angry. He's an ass – and he can kiss my natural-born black ass!' – Tameka Bush, *American Idol*, 2003

'I wouldn't touch Simon Cowell with a barge pole.' – Hayley, *Pop Idol*, 2003

'I was never one of Simon's priorities. Simon Cowell is Simon's priority.' – Steve Brookstein, *The X Factor* winner, 2004

'My mum's Jewish. My dad's Nigerian. Please, you can't not put me through. My mum will go mad. I've got a big voice. Don't say I'm not through, because you're mad! That's wrong. *The X Factor* is mad. I'm thirty-eight – this is it for me!' – Rowetta's plea to the judges, *The X Factor*, 2004

'Everybody looks at him as this menace but in reality, if you take what he's saying in the right way, and if you filter out all the silly comments he makes and focus on the

meaning of the comments, that can help you out a lot.' – Anthony Fedorov, *American Idol* finalist, 2004

'I could see what would have happened if I'd signed Simon Cowell's deal, which was for a shedload of money. I'd have been under the control of a marketing man who told me what to do and what to wear, what to sing and what to be. It would have driven me nuts.' – Darius Danesh, *Pop Idol*, 2003

'The first time I saw Simon, I just fell in love with the guy. He's so cool.' – Sara Nunes, *American Idol*, 2002

'Simon Cowell is like Simon Cowell. There's no other way to really describe it. He's a very funny little man.' – Diana DeGarmo, *American Idol*, 2004

'I know Simon Cowell can't sing and isn't talented, so he should just calm down and stop judging other people.' – Morwenna Marshall, *Pop Idol*, 2003

'You can't take anyone seriously who created The Spice Girls.' – Chris Neville Smith, *Pop Idol*, 2002

'If he believes in you, then you're laughing.' – Rowetta, *The X Factor*, 2004

'In real life, Simon is a gentleman with manners. He's just brutally honest and quite cruel for the effect of entertaining. He only didn't sign me up because I turned down his very gracious offer.' – Darius Danesh, *Pop Idol*, 2003

'You wouldn't know talent if it hit you in the face. You're a disgrace!' – Ben David Wynne, *The X Factor*, 2004

'I couldn't say anything bad about Simon Cowell because he's been all right to me so

far. I'm just wondering what the catch is.'
– Tabby, *The X Factor*, 2004

'What's your name? Simon Cowell.

Pull your trousers down to your waist.

You wouldn't know talent if it hit you in the face.

You're a disgrace!

You don't know shit,

Apart from bubble-gum pop, and that's it.

You think I really care about topping the charts?

Shove that commercial right up your arse!'
– Rap by Benjamin, *The X Factor*, 2004

'You'll be sorry!' – Tony Little after Simon dismissed him from *The X Factor*, 2005

BITING BACK:
THE JUDGES' DECISION IS FINAL

'I've fallen out with Simon many times. He's a little Hitler with a high waistband.'
Louis Walsh

'I don't know why Simon has to be so rude. Maybe he wasn't held enough as a child.' – Paula Abdul

'Simon's big flaw is that he is indecisive. He changes his mind. He's got a phenomenal gut instinct but he's never learnt to trust it.' – Pete Waterman

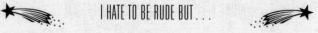
'Simon's a bit of a drag queen. I wouldn't be surprised if he dressed up in his spare time.' – Louis Walsh

'Simon thinks all women should be like blow-up dolls, have big tits and do whatever he says.' – Sharon Osbourne

'There is love there, and then there's times when I can't even stomach him.' – Paula Abdul

'Simon is a pompous little prick who walks like he has a stick stuck up his arse. In fact, I used to think he was a repressed homosexual.' – Sharon Osbourne

'His man boobs are bigger than mine.' – Paula Abdul

'In a strange way, I do like Simon. He can be quite charming. But he's the kind of bloke who would tell you he's got a big dick, the kind who would wear tight red Speedos on

the beach in the hope you might want to find out.' – Sharon Osbourne

'You don't argue with Simon. He has an opinion and it's not the same as yours. I don't know if that constitutes an argument.' – Pete Waterman.

'Simon is harmless. He knows how to push people's buttons, and it works for him and for the show. He doesn't physically hurt people, so if you adopt the old sticks-and-stones philosophy in dealing with him, you're pretty safe. I think he's sometimes like an adolescent who finds it funny when people embarrass or humiliate themselves.' – Paula Abdul

'People take the mickey out of the height of his waistband with justification. If his trousers were any higher, when he opened his flies, his nose would pop out. It's not his fault; he can't be over 5ft 2in.' – Nigel Lythgoe

'Simon said he thinks I fancy him. In fact, I'd rather have a giant lobster in my crotch than him! I'm not attracted to squeaky-clean men – I like a bit of rough.' – Sharon Osbourne

'Part of it's his personality, part of it's his English humour. You can say to someone in England, "Oh my God, you're fat – get off the TV!" and people will die laughing. [In the US], people will be like, "You know what? That wasn't really a nice thing to say." [His] criticism is only a small glimpse of what people will get, facing the public.' – Randy Jackson

'When you put me and Simon in a room together, the term "falling out" is not strong enough.' – Pete Waterman

'You've got to look for the glint in Simon's eyes sometimes, all right, because he is lovely at being provocative. He does things to spark people.' – Pete Waterman

'He is a huge egomaniac who doesn't know how to spot real talent.' – Louis Walsh

'He's a fucking wanker! I'm not going to leave the show because I work for ITV and not him, but he's pissed me off.' – Sharon Osbourne

'He always says I want him, and I don't want him. I don't want fungus, I don't want root canal and I don't want that.' – Paula Abdul

'He has the kind of eyes you see on dead fish at Billingsgate.' – Nigel Lythgoe

'Michelle McManus only sold one hundred thousand. It wasn't a case of Superman versus Batman; it was more like one of them is successful and the other one's a pudding. I still cannot understand how Simon Cowell could have said to her, "You're a breath of fresh air."'
– Pete Waterman

'There is no man more vain than Simon, but he does wear the same thing every day and he wears it tight on a body that's not necessarily the fittest on prime-time television.' – Ryan Seacrest

'Simon seems to get a surge out of trampling on people's dreams.' – Randy Jackson

'I'm not afraid to stand up to Simon. I understand he represents the ugliness of this business, but he also represents questioning the American dream – not just questioning it; crushing it – whereas I'm about hope.' – Paula Abdul

'I've known Simon for over twenty-five years and therefore I can tell him to stick his head up his arse and whistle. I'm the only one who can do that.' – Pete Waterman

I DON'T MEAN TO BE RUDE BUT . . .

'Fame doesn't turn people into monsters.
It enables them to become monsters.'
Simon Cowell

On Britney Spears: 'I actually don't find her sexy. I think anyone who puts a snake around her neck and thinks they're sexy has a weird idea of what guys actually like.'

'When I think of Madonna on stage now, it's like looking at my mum dancing at a wedding. She's in her forties and a mum. She doesn't shock me any more.'

On Jennifer Lopez: 'Anyone turning up at *Top of the Pops* with an entourage of seventy is just a joke. She represents everything I loathe about certain artists.'

'Chris Evans is a tosser. He is somebody who, when he was in a position of power, abused it. I met him when he was at Radio 1 and I desperately wanted to smack him in the mouth. He's a rude, arrogant little prick. I intensely despise the guy.'

'Beyoncé Knowles is the most ambitious artist on the planet. Look in her eyes and they're cold. She's like a steamroller. I find the whole thing really mystifying. She's not sexy, she hasn't got a great body and she's not a great singer.'

On Oasis (2002): 'Their latest offering was nothing like as good as "Wonderwall", and my acts [Will Young and Gareth Gates in the UK and Kelly Clarkson in the US] are going to be

number one in the UK and America this weekend. Oasis aren't!'

On Blur: 'They made some great records once.'

On Michael Barrymore: 'He should accept that he's history. I always thought he had a self-destruct button. He took celebrity too seriously.'

On the BBC TV show *Strictly Come Dancing*: 'I sat there literally open-mouthed. It's one of the strangest shows I've ever seen in my life. You've got so many terrible dancers in there. It's car-crash TV. If I was seventy-five years old and I was sitting at home with my slippers on, I'd watch it. If I was below seventy, I'd watch *The X-Factor*.

On singer Shakira: 'I don't understand a word that girl is singing. She is comparing her breasts with mountains in her first song. What the hell is that about?'

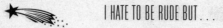

On Victoria Beckham: 'Her last album was rubbish. She needs to rethink her career.'

'If Kelly Osbourne auditioned for the show, she wouldn't get through the first round.'

'I was a fan of Britney [Spears]'s early records. When I see her doing the whole Madonna thing, it's rather like watching your little sister putting on make-up for the first time. You sort of think, "Oh, God, don't!"'

On his girlfriend, Terri Seymour: 'She is a dreadful driver, the worst driver I have ever come across in my life. She still doesn't realise you have to drive on the opposite side of the road in America.'

Mick Hucknall: 'I just find him very irritating.

On Robbie Williams: 'He's one of the world's top artists, but the problem for him

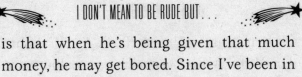
is that when he's being given that much money, he may get bored. Since I've been in the States, doing *American Idol*, Robbie has been trying to crack the market. I don't think it matters for him, but I'm bigger than him over there.'

On Jessica Simpson: 'The odd thing about the music industry is that here's a girl whose career wasn't exactly on fire and then she goes on television, pretends that she thinks that Chicken of the Sea is actually chicken, and on the back of that sells two million records. It's weird, isn't it? I have a certain respect for her, because she is like an ambitious wolf.'

On Madonna: 'I haven't liked any of her records in the last five years. In fact, there's no way I could even begin to hum her last three songs. My message to you, Madonna, is give up!'

On Kym Marsh (August 2003): 'I'm afraid her record label won't get their investment back. There's no way she'll sell millions of records. Kym will be over in nine months.'

On *Big Brother* contestant Jade Goody: 'Jade was pretending she was thick. She wasn't thick, and she knew what she was doing. Jade knew where East Anglia was; she was just playing up to the cameras.'

On Geri Halliwell's 2004 single 'Ride It': 'If I was her record label and that video arrived on my desk, I'd throw it in the bin!'

On Mariah Carey's comeback: 'Was there one? I'm not sure if anyone cares any more. If you're going to come back, it has to be with an awesome record, like Kylie Minogue's.'

On Michael Jackson (2003): 'How the mighty fall. It really is the final straw for this guy. Just when you think things can't get any worse, he holds his baby out of a window. It's actually quite unbelievable.'

On Justin Timberlake and Britney Spears: 'If I were him, I'd be playing the field at this point. And I don't find her sexy. Actually, I find the whole thing rather dreary.'

'If Duncan from Blue was signed to me, I would tell him to calm his ego down. I can't stand people who believe their own hype.'

On Whitney Houston: 'If she was a friend of mine and she ever asked me for advice – hard to imagine – I'd say, "Dump the husband!"'

On Geri Halliwell: 'I just don't think she's got it. It all looks and sounds very juvenile. At the end of the day, it's about selling albums, and I don't know anyone who'd want to buy her's.'

To John McEnroe: 'I don't like rude people.'

'If Mick Hucknall was a plumber and looked the way he does, he'd find it pretty hard to score.'

'Justin Timberlake a heartthrob? I really don't get it. Justin is a white boy who has tried to make himself black over the years, so you get the impression sometimes that he wants to be something he's not.'

On Liz Hurley: 'I don't think anyone courted publicity more fiercely, but when she achieves what she wants, she wants to know why the press is invading her privacy. Well, don't wear a fucking dress that's held together with safety pins!'

On Courtney Love: 'I look at her and think she's grubby.'

On The Spice Girls: 'Geri can't sing. I don't rate her as a solo artist. She was great in The Spice Girls because of her ambition,

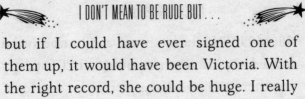
but if I could have ever signed one of them up, it would have been Victoria. With the right record, she could be huge. I really like her.'

'People say that success has changed this artist or that one, but I find that success rarely changes anyone. Rather, it gives them the power to be what they always were: assholes.'

After Jack Osbourne called Simon a slimeball: 'I'd be amazed if Jack Osbourne could spell "slimeball", never mind understand it!'

After former Westlife member Brian McFadden said boy bands were dead (September 2004): 'There's a market for everybody. Pop music from boy bands and girl bands will definitely make a strong comeback, so people like Brian McFadden should just go away and stop yakking about things they don't know about.'

★

'Victoria [Beckham] should definitely not be working with hip-hop producers. They go together like chocolate ice-cream and onions.'

'Tony Blair would make a great pop star because he's one of the most ambitious people in the world. His ambition would outweigh his talent but, he would be able to reason away the fact that he couldn't sing.'

'J-Lo isn't a singer; she's a brand, one hundred per cent about making money.'

On Sharon Osbourne moving in next door to him: 'She's just far enough away to fly off on her broomstick.'

Following a break-in at Sharon Osborne's house: 'It was well worth giving away the diamonds for that amount of press coverage.'

On Michael Jackson: 'Next!'

On Prince William: 'He's got the looks and class of a real star. I don't know whether he can sing or not, but let's face it, that's not always a problem.'

On Bob Dylan: 'Too ugly, too boring, too whiny and too serious.'

On Abi Titmuss: 'She's just an overweight girl with big tits and isn't as attractive as Jordan.'

To David Hasselhoff: 'David, the problem with you is that you are incredibly precious.'

On Gary Barlow of Take That: 'Fire the fat one and I'll sign the band!'

On Cliff Richard's 'Millennium Prayer': 'I found the whole thing revolting. I couldn't listen to the record – it wound me up, it was so premeditated.'

CELEBRITIES BITE BACK

'Simon has a real attitude problem and I think
he is way too cruel.'
Mariah Carey

'I'VE got no time for Simon Cowell. I really
think the show's all about being rude to
people.' – Phil Collins

'I think that he's pompous. I think that he's
arrogant. So my feelings about him, and the
way that I address him on air, are very real.'
– Ryan Seacrest, *American Idol* host

'I don't find him attractive and I wouldn't

recommend him as a boyfriend. I think he'd be a sod to date. He's powerful and he's funny, witty and confident, but I don't fancy him.' – Kate Thornton, *The X Factor* host

'We really wanted him to judge our competition and were prepared to pay any amount to get him. However, he never seemed that interested. He never returned our calls, anyway. He would have been great, as he is so camp on TV.' – The organiser for the Mr Gay UK awards

'His personality away from the camera is exactly what you see on camera. He's honest, he can be nasty. He'll say what he thinks constantly, and sometimes you don't want to hear it.' – Terri Seymour

'He was then and he is now the funniest person I've ever met. Just hilarious.' – Simon's former girlfriend Mandy Perriment

'Simon Cowell wouldn't dare be nasty to me, though. I may not be Lily Savage any more but I've still got a sharp tongue, believe me.' – Paul O'Grady

'He always had a good body. He used to hang out of his window in his vest, eyeing up the girls walking by. I always knew he was going to go places.' – Arlene Phillips

'I spent years trying to be sexy enough for Simon. I think I failed. He certainly didn't shower me with money or jewels. One year he bought me a lamp for my birthday. Another year he got me a kettle.' – Sinitta

'I kinda like that nasty British guy.' – US President George Bush

'Simon Cowell needs my mum on that panel. I mean, who else would you be watching it for, if not her?' – Jack Osbourne

'My first impression of Cowell was that he's a really honest man.' – David Miller, Il Divo

★

'I'm in love with Simon Cowell. Girls love bastards!' – Susannah Constantine

★

'I only disagree with him ten per cent of the time.' – Lulu

★

'That dreadful man' – Her Majesty the Queen

★

'Simon strives to be plain nasty. He doesn't appreciate what success has brought him: the car, the teeth, the best hair that money can buy from the specialist clinics.'
– Nigel Lythgoe

★

'He should be melted down and turned into glue.' – Chris Martin, Coldplay

★

'Let's not forget that whatever anyone thinks of Simon Cowell or Robson and Jerome, people did laugh, but the industry took it very seriously because we made the industry lots of money.' – Robson Green

'Simon's ego is so out of control. He likes to keep me in check by reminding me my career is down to him and has absolutely nothing to do with me.' – Terri Seymour

'I'll break his fucking nose! I want to know where Simon buys his boots so I can fill them full of shit and throw them at him!' – Ozzy Osbourne

'I'd like to punch that geek. I'd like to punch him now, this minute.' – Des Lynam

'I think he's repulsive. I want to just slap him. I'd love to give him a big bitch-slap.' – Billy Connolly

'I would take his advice and whatever he said and tell him to shove it.' – Britney Spears

'Simon's a tart. He's done everything from date my best friend when we were engaged, and he tried to date my twin sister when we were engaged.' – Sinitta

'If he has a less expensive car, it's a problem. If your shoes are more expensive, it's an issue. If your house has more bedrooms, it's a problem. That's Simon.' – Ryan Seacrest, *American Idol* host

'His persona thrives on whipping up controversy. You can't be Mr Nasty if you don't get a reaction, so bruised pride, rising hackles and pissed-off celebs with badly punctured egos are Cowell's meat and drink.' – Vanessa Feltz

'Simon Cowell's got an opinion about everyone. I mean, he talked about Robbie [Williams] and said how rubbish he thinks Robbie is! That's just ridiculous; the guy's sold millions of albums.' – Kym Marsh

★

'You can't talk about commitment with Simon. He puts his hands over his ears and trills, "La, la, la," like a child.' – Terri Seymour

'Simon Cowell has seen his earnings increase to £33.5 million a year. Is that just from crushing kids?' – MSP Jim Sheridan

'I think you're great, but you're kind of short and a bit hairy.' Kate Thornton, *The X Factor* host

'If the world thinks Simon Cowell is representative of people in the music industry, they're wrong. Simon Cowell is the guy that discovered Sinitta. I rest my case. It's a joke.' – Andy Taylor, Duran Duran

'I like Simon very much. We deliver his newspapers every day and he doesn't discriminate between rich and poor. He's a very kind man.' – Simon's local newsagent in Kensington, London

'I wouldn't say he's my best friend but I accept him for what he is: the baddie in a pantomime.' – Ozzy Osbourne

'It ought to be a crime to publicly humiliate contestants on *American Idol*.' – Pat Boone

'He's very generous to my girls, and while he may be Mr Nasty outside, they consider him to be Mr Wonderful.' – Peter Stringfellow

'It was nice to meet someone worse behaved than me.' – Abi Titmuss

'He's arrogant, he's pompous and he believes that everything he says is right. He drives you crazy.' – Ryan Seacrest, *American Idol* host

'He's honest. I think the thing we love about him is that he's saying what we're all thinking.' – Gloria Estefan

'I'm not a fan of Simon Cowell and his brand of manufactured pop. I hate these music reality shows that tell you there has to be a choreographer, a voice coach and a hair stylist. It's crap.' – Alex Kapranos, Franz Ferdinand

'I think he says things that are at times a bit too harsh and could probably convey them in a different light so that they don't crush a young person's dream.' – Ryan Seacrest, *American Idol* host

'This man gave Robson and Jerome a fortune for destroying a bunch of old classics and we're expected to believe he has an ear for music. As the saying goes, this fish is four days old and I'm not buying!' – Boy George

'Simon is living proof that money obviously doesn't buy you style.' – Ant

'It would have been a dictatorship. No matter what anyone says, Simon Cowell would tell

you what to do.' – James Bourne on why Busted didn't sign with Simon's record company

★

'If I ran into him, I'd give him a piece of my mind. I think shows like *Pop Idol* take away the heart and soul of music.' – Alicia Keys

★

'[Simon] is just a weak caricature of himself and has nothing to say.' – Zack Werner, *Canadian Idol* judge

★

'He's much older and shorter than he'd have us believe, and he totters around on these stupid Cuban heels. They're bespoke and he bulk-buys them. He spends thousands of pounds on his high heels and they make him look ridiculous. He's that conceited. I've also caught him with a round brush, blow-drying his hair.' – Kate Thornton, *The X Factor* host

★

'I remember once that we did a photo shoot for a magazine and Simon was going through the photos. Brian [McFadden] was on honeymoon in Mauritius at that time, but Simon called him up and told him he looked fat.' – Mark Feehilly, Westlife

'Do I like Simon Cowell? You bet I do! In this world of spin doctors, lickspittles, jobsworths and do-gooders, he's one of the very few people on the planet who actually tell the truth.' – Vanessa Feltz

'I hate the show he's on. I like it that the guy has some balls, and I appreciate he always says what he feels, but it's pathetic that people sit around and watch shows like that on TV.' – Tommy Lee

'He would enjoy his life a lot more if he would just come out. I reckon he's dying to.' – Ozzy Osbourne

'Simon's never told me off in the five years I worked for him. He's great at giving praise.' – Nikki Watkins, Simon's former PA

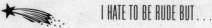

'If he spoke to us the way he does to those kids on TV, we'd kill him. We're too mad and old for that. We're not youngsters who he can manipulate.' – Sebastien Izambard, Il Divo

'I didn't want my mom to do *The X Factor*. It was pretty yellow-bellied to go on a show with a guy who's said so many nasty things about her family and kids. But she went on, and the show's interesting. Simon Cowell is a slimeball.' – Jack Osbourne

'Simon is arrogant, vain and funny, and the entertainment industry would be a much better place if there were more people like him.' – Kate Thornton, *The X Factor* host

TABLOID TALES

'Simon Cowell's judgements may be stern, but they are sharp and his stardom attests to the fact that, deep down, Americans still hunger for the truth. Funny that it takes a Brit to remind us.'

The Wall Street Journal

'Cowell is both defiantly laddish and magnificently queenly – Dale Winton meets Priapus.' – Simon Hattenstone, *The Guardian*

'Cowell is annoying, smug, snide, rude, vain, mean and prancing, with strange hair and a twisted smile.' – *The Sunday Express*

'Cowell is the greatest British export since The Beatles.' – *USA Today*

★

'You can't buy style, and even if you could, Simon Cowell wouldn't know which shop to go to. He might call his black roundneck sweater "trademark"; I call it lazy and insecure. Wearing the same clothes all the time is for people who don't know who they are.' – Bethan Cole, *The Sunday Times*

★

'The ascendancy of Simon Cowell goes to show that Americans remain, after all these centuries, unduly impressed by a British accent.' – Ken Tucker, *CNN*

★

'Will the real Simon Cowell ever stand up?' – *The New York Post*

★

'I salute Cowell as a TV hero. As indeed have the Americans, since he went stateside and abused their pop wannabes. After all,

120

someone has to do it.' – Gerard Gilbert, *The Independent*

'Simon Cowell is the Barry Goldwater of reality TV: in your heart, you know he's right.' – James Poniewozik, *Time* magazine

'If Satan ever retires, Simon can take the job.' – *Mancow*

'Cowell is the new pantomime villain of the music industry.' – *The Daily Telegraph*

'In an age when parents aren't able to confront their children's shortcomings, it sometimes seems like Cowell is the only one who will.' – Alexandra Wolfe, *The New York Times*

'Simon Cowell has changed the way in which we think about television in the US.' – *Time*

'Cowell's affected nastiness toward contestants who don't have talent has become so

predictable he's little more than a fourth-rate insult comic. And not even slightly funny.' – Scott D Pierce, *Deseret Morning News*

'All men to whom women are instantly drawn have one thing in common: they listen to you as if you are the only person in the room, and heaven knows, Cowell does. He is charismatic, articulate, bright and funny.' – Jaci Stephen, *The Mail on Sunday*

'Simon, you're a villain, not because of your bitchy, caustic put-downs towards spotty, deluded kids, but because you still hold your smug head high above your shoulders, believing you can tell us what music we should buy and what constitutes a real star or singer.' – Ed Harcourt, *The Independent*

'A good celebrity is someone who knows that they have a ridiculous job. They understand that being a celebrity is actually stupid and have fun with it. Simon Cowell, for example,

I think has a lot of fun being Simon Cowell. And his judgment is pretty bang on, apart from *Zig & Zag* and *The Power Rangers*.'
– *The Independent*

'Cowell maintains he is an enormously open and honest person. He is, but he is also impossible to fathom. And he is never happy with what he has. The house, the girlfriends, the millions, the success – none of it is enough. He always wants more.' – Rebecca Hardy, *The Mail on Sunday*

'I wanna kick his butt! He's just too much. There's something about the guy. I think he can accomplish what he wants. You just don't have to be that mean. It's painful to watch.'
– Donnie Deutsch, US TV host

'Cowell is an enigma. He's the antithesis of the "You're beautiful and talented just the way you are, but you might not want to give up the day job" political correctness this country once fawned over. The song "Cruel to be Kind" could have been written for him because he's the man who, literally, tells it like it is.' – Hannah Jones, *Western Mail*

'The real genius here, though, is Simon as judge, jury and executioner. He takes this talent show where no talent show has ever gone before. Simon Cowell is Wile E. Coyote in disguise, and how entertaining would the Roadrunner have been without him?' – Gully Guy, *Elites TV*

'Fox Television needs to lighten up on that white concealer under his eyes. It's supposed to reduce on-camera puffiness, but it sometimes makes Cowell look like a raccoon.' – Phillip Swann, *HDTV*

'He's funny, he's charming and he's quite good-looking. He's got twinkly eyes and he's very charismatic.' – Ian Hyland, *The Sunday Mirror*

★

'Simon Cowell puts his mouth where the money is, earning a king's ransom on *American Idol* by using his tongue as a machete. He wears muscle shirts to accessorise his overall vanity. But sitting next to Paula Abdul is enough to make anyone feel completely superior.' – Ed Bark, *Dallas Morning News*

'The beauty of Simon is that there's no deeper, sinister side to him; he's just a man who says what he thinks. He's a tough cookie and could be a real bastard, but from our experience, he's not. He's a straight talker who's good fun to be around.' – Stewart Morris, producer

'Simon's ego is so large it is the only man-made object that can be seen from space' – *The Los Angeles Times*

'I've fallen out with Simon many times. He's a little Hitler with a high waistband.' – Louis Walsh

COMPETING — NOBODY DOES IT BETTER

'I'm very, very, very competitive. And I'm only happy when I'm winning.'

Simon Cowell

'IF I believe someone can do something better than me, then I'll take a back seat, but when it comes to a lot of the things I do in my job, I honestly believe I do it better than other people.'

★

'I remember when I officially became a millionaire. It was what I'd always dreamed of. I was skiing when this contract arrived

that meant I was officially there. I felt nothing. I thought, "OK, this is not just about money. There's more to it." Playing the game is part of the buzz. It is a game and playing it is fun.'

★

'I'm not interested in being a TV celebrity for the sake of it. I'm only interested in being more successful than anyone else.'

★

'I don't need to work but I love it. I'll only retire when I lose the plot.'

★

'I know exactly the people who are praying for my downfall on a nightly basis. In a way, it drives me on even more.'

★

'I still think I'm the best spotter of talent in the country.'

★

On Sharon Osbourne winning the Most Popular Expert award at the UK's National Television awards, 2005: 'Sharon kind of took the gloss off the evening. I'm not a giving person; I'm a receiving person. I still haven't heard the last of it from Kelly. She loved the fact that her mum beat me.'

'Of course I'm motivated by money. Tell me who isn't. I've always taken the view that nobody should do something for nothing. It's just a rule I've always had for myself.'

'I do not think of myself and the word "stardom" in the same sentence. I think I've become very well known but I don't consider myself to be a celebrity or a star at all. I have the same friends and go to the same places. I certainly don't walk around in dark glasses with an entourage. That's not going to happen. You have to keep your feet on the ground. You can't take it too seriously.'

'The only thing that makes me happy is money. If it could pour on me every day like a shower, I would lie in that shower for hours. I'm very motivated by money: I just love it.'

'The truth is that there are times when I am not happy. You put your heart and soul into something, and sometimes you can make mistakes, but you pick yourself up and start again.'

'If you asked me to describe the past two or three years, I'd say they've been fun, but it's just been target practice. I want more.'

'No one should feel embarrassed about admitting they're in this for the money. I don't do projects to be remembered in fifty years' time or to make a cultural difference. If I want art, I'll buy it. Anyone who comes to my label to work is there to make as much money as possible.'

'I've had to be ruthless. That's just the way it is. I always will be. If I want something strongly enough, I'll get it, no matter what.'

'I'm quite a trusting person, but I trust myself over anyone else.'

'I'm very interesting, and I'm enough of an egotist to be honest about that.'

'I'm verging on obsessive about work, which isn't good. I had a holiday because I was so tired and I said to my girlfriend, "Mobiles off." After two hours, I was twitching.'

'Only those people who aren't doing so well criticise my acts.'

'I wanted to be in control of my destiny, and that's what television has done for me, but I have no desire for fame. If it all stopped tomorrow and I had to go behind the scenes again, I'd be happy. People are already sick to death of me.'

'Money is fantastic. It's the best thing in the world. It changes you as a person; it gives you confidence. I first appreciated how much money I had a year and a half ago. I'd watched a documentary on a single mother who had to borrow £250 at Christmas for presents and a hamper and then had to pay back £45 each month for the following year.'

★

'I don't care what people say about me. My only motivation is to be successful and make money. It's the only motivation I've ever had.'

★

'If you've got a big mouth and you're controversial, you're going to get attention – and I do.'

★

'I love [UK TV show] *The Office*. I just got the first season. I am literally addicted to that show. I relate to the boss, David Brent [played by Ricky Gervais]. We are both unpopular.'

'The industry I work in is very fickle. Pop artists have a short shelf life. I'd always be thinking, "Am I going to find the next Westlife? Will I be offered the next Spice Girls?" Now I have a business that can grow, so in five or ten years I won't be relying on *Pop Idol* or *American Idol* to give me my status.'

'I'm well known for being a judge on a TV show, and that doesn't give me any talent. If you're famous, you have to have a talent, and I don't consider sitting on a TV show and criticising people to be a talent. And no, I can't sing or dance.'

'I am quite miserable because I'm never satisfied with what I've got. You're always looking for that next high, and that's what I would define as happiness.'

'If someone wants to come into my office, they've got to accept that I'm going to tell them the truth. If they don't want to hear that, there are a lot of other people in this business who will tell them whatever they want to hear.'

'I've never been shy of money. I'm in this business to make a profit.'

'I think you have to judge everything based on your personal taste. And if that means being critical about people, so be it.'

'People don't come up to me and say, "You're so horrible." They come up and say, "Thank you for your honesty."'

'In this job you need that weird combination of arrogance and insecurity.'

'The music industry is a culture awash with sycophants and yes, men. There's far too much decorum and protocol. My harsh criticism may be tough on some people, but in the main it tends to have a positive effect. Most importantly, it separates the wannabes from the real stars, and does so as swiftly and uncomfortably as possible.'

'Music and TV have come unstuck recently, led by the ponytail brigade who come in with charts and figures and say, "This is the age category you should be appealing to." How the fuck do they know what I like?'

'If there's one thing I've learned, it's not to look back at my mistakes – and I've made plenty of them.'

'If I look at the past, I'm on five per cent of what I want to achieve.'

'The fear of failure is horrific. My self-esteem is bound up with my work.'

'I think I've always been vile in real life. If I'm not annoying anybody, I'm not doing my job properly.'

'I don't see the point of doing anything that makes you sound like a dog. That's why I hate yodelling.'

THE SEX FACTOR

*'I think most people mistake lust for love.
My feelings of being in love were mostly when I was
younger, out of control and lusting after somebody.'*
Simon Cowell

'I know it sounds pathetic but I'm always terrified that, if I make a commitment, a week later I'll meet somebody else. I've never really had the feeling with any girl that this is "The One". It's like when you order a black car and the week before it comes, you see a silver car and go, "I wish I'd ordered a silver car."'

'I can't criticise anyone who has written a story about an ex-girlfriend. I can, however, criticise some of the girls because there are one or two who have said things that are just lies. There is one in particular, called Debbie, who only did a kiss and tell on me because I went to bed with her and didn't phone her again. The really cruel people in this world are girls, not guys.'

'I don't play rugby, I don't drink beer, I don't hang out in pubs, I take an interest in what I wear and I'm forty-three-years-old and single, but if I were gay, I would happily admit it. I'm not gay, but if I didn't know me and I met me, I probably would think, "Yeah, he's gay."'

'I don't care about being loved. I'm loved by my family, and a few people like me on TV, but that's not love. I never wanted to be on TV. I couldn't care less.'

'I'm pragmatic. I don't expect everyone I date to jump into bed with me. They don't have to be a lap dancer, although that does break the ice. Women seem to like me – I don't know why that is. But I've been turned down by girls millions of times. It's humiliating.'

On having children: 'I've never had the need to have another me.'

'It's true to say I've always been comfortable in the company of women and I have got myself a bit of a reputation these days. I can still remember my first crush, when I was five, on a girl called Amanda.'

'I don't want babies the same way I wouldn't want a puppy.'

'Women just come up to me and kiss me. They've even been known to put their hands down my trousers before.'

'Nasty is sexier than nice.'

'If I'm comfortable with somebody, like my girlfriend Terri, I'll argue. If I'm not comfortable, I become icily polite, and that's not a great place to be.'

'If I were to hazard a guess, I'd say I'd had somewhere between seventy and a hundred women, but they seem to go as quickly as they arrive. I think I have a bigger sex drive than average.' – Simon in 2003

'Terri is very understanding about my work. We've never had that uncomfortable conversation where she says, "Simon, I want kids." I've persuaded her that a puppy is a better alternative.'

On his parents: 'From the second they woke up to the second they fell asleep, they would talk. They never shut up. It used to make me laugh. But a marriage like that is very rare.'

'I am a hedonist at heart. I love the uncertainty and the challenge. I'm also exceptionally competitive and ambitious. It is relentless,

relentless, relentless. I can't help it. Sometimes I'm glad. Sometimes I wish I wasn't like that all the time. I can never switch off. Sometimes I wish I could find peace, but somehow I don't think I'm ever going to change.'

'Controlling a relationship is when you play with someone's mind, and I've never done that.'

'I like to spoil my girlfriends, mentally, because I try to turn all my girlfriends into brats.'

'Since I've been with Terri [Seymour], I've been shouted and screamed at like I've never been shouted and screamed at in my life.'

On plastic surgery: 'I'd make it compulsory for every woman over forty.'

'I love being pampered, but I hate having my photo taken. I'm shy, believe it or not.'

'Valentine's Day is my worst time of year. I find the whole thing appalling. It's ghastly. That one night of the year that you have to be romantic. The teddy bears and the flowers – urgh! It's just a horrible thing. I find symbolic romantic things naff. I don't want to buy people flowers; I'd rather buy them a car. I'm not romantic, but I make up for it in other areas.'

On his US dating TV show, *Cupid*: 'I wanted to make it real. There is nothing more devastating to a guy than walking across a bar to meet a girl and having her friends demolish him. This is not going to be a sweet fairy tale. There's a bite to it. Dating is cruel. Anyone who says the dating process isn't cruel doesn't know what planet they're on.'

'There are a lot of celebrities out there who make a very good living out of being perceived as family men when they're not. I despise that. If you're going to sleep around, then admit it. I love women, I adore them. I've always been comfortable in their company, and I think that's why some people think I'm gay.'

'I was broke about fifteen years ago, and since I've met Terri I've become broke again.'

'I told Terri to buy a terrapin instead of having a baby because they can be affectionate and we'll have a little pet, but it didn't go down too well.'

'I've always loved women, which is why I find it so odd that people say that I'm gay. It doesn't annoy me. To me, it's nothing to be ashamed of.'

'I've dated my fair share of attractive male-model types, and while Simon is good-looking, what I find really sexy about him is his character and his sense of humour.'
– Terri Seymour

ALL ABOUT YOU

The following are letters written by American girls and boys and posted onto the Simon Cowell University website (http://simonpics.com/simoncowelluniversity/). Health warning: some of these letters could induce severe vomiting.

'Dear Sir. My last boyfriend and I only went out for about one month. He is an ass. Mr Cowell has left great expectations and high standards, which will probably be hard for anyone to live up to. In no way am I only interested in money or furthering my career. As far as I can tell, I'm loving, trustworthy, gentle, patient and intelligent, with a keen *sense of humor and quick wit. If I try hard enough, I could probably squeeze some kindness out of myself. I would be more than willing to sign a pre-nuptial agreement. I am very organised and I pay a lot of attention to detail. I also have a passion for burning white Armani sweaters.' – Brittany*

'Dear Sirs. Starting at the ripe old age of eight, I received my first proper kiss under the slide in the school playground. Since that day I have been practising my kissing abilities with the sole goal of linking lips with Simon Cowell. SCU is my university of choice because I feel that my past reflects a true dedication to the cause. I have travelled the world, and with this comes an understanding on frequent travelling and packing of suitcases, which I feel is an asset to Mr Cowell. I also am well trained in cooking for the picky eater and can modify any food to be plain and devoid of excessive flavourings. I also hold a wines and spirits diploma, which was a practical course involving

sampling many wines, spirits and other, lesser forms of intoxicating liquids. I am able to function for weeks on end on four to five hours of sleep and thus have an ability to be on call, should Mr Cowell ever need any assistance. I am well trained in yoga and, despite my small frame, I am fully toned, dare I say 125lb of pure muscle, and I would like the opportunity to compare/share muscles with Mr. Cowell.' – Clary

'Dear SCU. I met your president, Mr Simon Cowell, one time in Nashville during auditions for American Idol 2. *I was totally blown away when I actually got to shake the hand of The Great One and also was lucky enough to mingle with him for a few minutes. For just those couple minutes, I thought life could get no better – until today, when I saw this, Simon Cowell University. For the last three years I have spent most of my time online, searching for new sites to read up and look at pictures of Mr Cowell. To be able to have the satisfaction to*

attend such a grand college such as this one would be a dream come true.' – lbondchick

'Sirs. I strongly feel that I have the necessary qualifications to be a full professor of Special Education at Simon Cowell University. I have had years of experience in dealing with those with special needs. For this reason, I feel that I am well qualified to teach the obsessive/compulsive or delusional applicants to the university.' – Petmom

'Dear Sirs. I would like to apply to Simon Cowell University. Why? Well, I'll tell you why: because I love Mr. Cowell more than anything. I actually love him but for someone else, Paula Abdul. I mean, those two DO love each other a LOT. I hope to get in the university. I will study Simon Cowell's subjects and do great!' – Simonized

'Dear Sir. It is quite clear that we are all put on this Earth to worship one man, and this man is

Simon Cowell. Here's the real reason you should let me into SCU: I spent, like, an hour of my life writing this God-forsaken essay, and if that's not enough, I have enclosed a picture of Him with which to bribe you.' – Katie

'Dear Sirs. I have been loyal to him since American Idol first came on. Ever since, I haven't loved anyone more or even close. I love Simon Cowell more than everything you can imagine and more! I watch all AI episodes because of him. I have no interest in his money, whatsoever. All I want is to have fun with him and be loyal to him for the rest of my life. I would never cheat on him or make him unhappy or bored! I would always have something new to tell him, and would be happy to do what he feels like doing! I will keep him company on his best and worst moments, and whenever he needs me I will certainly be there for him! I will dedicate all the time I have to him, no matter what gets in the way! That is what will make me a great Cowell woman!' – Becca

'I admire Simon for his virility, but I am not a promiscuous person myself. I only venture into relationships with stable, honest and hardworking men, and this is why I love Simon so much. He is a business mastermind who is not ashamed of admitting his love for money. I wish to attend SCU to further educate myself in the world of Simon, and I would love to learn about him surrounded by like-minded people. The further study of Simon intrigues me, and I am filled with enthusiasm at learning about the man himself. I propose to study Physiology.'
– Lindsey P

★

'Ever since Simon was drawn to my attention on the very first episode of Pop Idol, I knew that his rather high waistband wouldn't stop me from loving him, as for what I envisioned there was no need to bring trousers into the equation. Over the episodes, my love for this beautiful man has expanded at an alarming rate, so much that by the end of the first series

I knew I would not be able to die happy unless I had met him at least once in my life. I then went about the procedure of applying for the second series of Pop Idol *in my haste to declare my love to him.*

'After that, I dedicated my life to getting through to see the judges in any way, shape or form that I could. Many months of hard work and gruelling singing went on in my room, my shower and even in the street. When I had finally set my heart on a song ("Toucha Toucha Toucha Touch Me"), I really couldn't decide on an outfit, so I thought it best to leave that part of the process out and just go in my underwear. I thought that Simon wouldn't mind, and how many people can boast that Simon Cowell has seen them in their underwear? So off I toddled to London to woo him and so I got up, dedicated my song to him and then left the room in a great hurry for fear of fainting. However, in my brief (get it? brief?) exchange of words between us, I finally knew what my purpose in life was: to love, honour and obey

that heavenly creature that was sitting just a few yards in front of me.

'So now I turn to you, oh great and wondrous university of The Great Heavenly Creature that was brought down from on high. Please help me to prepare for my life-long vocation. I know at times it will be tough, but with your guidance I could become a top stalker of the highest degree.' – Fifi the Great

'Dear Sirs. I wish to be admitted to the Simon Cowell University because Simon Cowell rocks my world. His personality is so sexy and intriguing. I feel I have good experience in areas such as cooking and massage. I love to travel and I am a former figure skater, which means I am very flexible. (Good for meeting Mr Cowell's needs!) Simon occupies my life; every magazine, every internet search and every small clip is treasured. You should see my video tape collection. It is insane. I am in love with this man so much that I slept out in Minute Maid Park in Houston to audition for

him. I can't even sing but, hey, that didn't stop me. I had to try and see him. I didn't complete my task of getting to him, so I think some education at SCU would help. "Obsessed with Simon" is an understatement. I have to go to SCU because Simon is my dream man. Admit me to the university and I will be able to accomplish my goal of pleasing, loving and experiencing Simon Cowell!' – Kelly

'We are not worthy!' – Rachel S

'There is love there, and then there's times when I can't
even stomach him.' – Paula Abdul

PART THREE

THE RUDE FACTOR AND HOW TO GET IT

MAD COWELL DISEASE

IT is a sad fact that there are many people around the world who suffer from Simon Cowell-related mental illnesses. The most common forms are those of delusion. For example:

- People believing they are Simon Cowell;
- People thinking that Simon Cowell is in love with them;
- People believing they will die if they don't see Simon on television at least eighteen times a week;

- People believing that Simon is actually a member of their own family;
- People who start to see their family members beginning to metamorphose into Simon.

Anyone who suffers from these types of problems might well benefit from reading this book, having group therapy or, perhaps, learning how to deal with the problem by turning negative Simon thoughts into positives. Remember: the first step to recovery is to admit you have a problem.

THOUGHT TRANSFERENCE

There are those who, immediately after watching Simon on television, suddenly feel empowered to be rude or nasty. They become confident and bold, thinking they're able to take on the world. While this kind of reaction is understandable, it is also dangerous. It could be seen as a form of thought transference, and in the same way Simon may well use this method to get people to vote for his acts. The main problem is that this is only a short-term fix; once the screen image of him has gone, the viewers' rude powers diminish and any attempt to try and emulate his sarcastic wit will normally end in disaster.

Do you ever feel that you *are* Simon Cowell? Do you believe you could actually be as rude, arrogant and nasty as him but don't really have the guts to change? You might even have got as far as practising in front of the mirror while suffering from Simon Cowell-based sensory hallucinations, manifested most often by a compulsion to pose as Simon on the Internet and converse with other fans or to deliberately start an argument with a family member or best friend in the hope of delivering a really crushing put-down or insult. But then, just when you're about to deliver the cruel punchline, you either forget what you were

about to say or, worse, stutter and it comes out all wrong. This is simply because you are *not* Simon Cowell.

Anyone can learn to be *like* Simon, but you must first learn what rudeness is and how to use it to improve your life. (Note: Please remember when attempting to be rude that you are *not* Simon Cowell. Likewise, it is suggested that you do not use his name, imitate his voice or try to dress like him.)

THE DEFINITION OF RUDENESS

So what is rudeness? Most thesauruses will provide you with the following synonyms of the adjective 'rude': impertinent, ill-mannered, insolent, blunt, brusque, churlish, surly, gruff, crass, arrogant, supercilious. Most of these thesauruses, however, were compiled before Cowell (BC), so what I refer to as SSR (the Simon Style of Rudeness) is more accurately defined as a state of being impudent or arrogantly self-confident.

Impudent, yes. Arrogant, yes. But the self-confidence aspect sets Simon apart and enables him to be outrageously rude and get away with it. Your very first lesson in your quest for Rudeness is:

I MUST BE SELF-CONFIDENT

Nobody can be rude and hope to get away with it unless they have self-confidence in abundance.

Have you ever heard Simon stutter? Have you ever heard him fluff a rude line on a television show? I don't think so. That's because being rude comes naturally to Simon. He already possesses the Rude Factor in huge quantities. However, like painting and ballroom dancing, anyone can learn to be rude and get away with it by first understanding the ground rules and then learning how to hone their technique.

RUDE AWAKENING

As I mentioned at the beginning of this book, anyone can be rude but it takes class to be rude and get away with it. Shouting and screaming at someone isn't rude; it's abusive. If you want to adopt the SSR, you'll first need to familiarise yourself with the five key components necessary in order to be rude with impunity:

- Self-confidence;
- Wit;
- Timing;
- Body language;
- Vocabulary and tone of voice.

These are the essential ingredients that will give you the Rude Factor. To master the art, you must learn to embrace these on the road to rudeness. To make this easier to understand, here are some examples of how Simon uses these five key attributes when being rude.

SELF-CONFIDENCE

'I think most people I know have rude thoughts. They think mean things. I'm much more comfortable with somebody telling me to my face the way they feel about me, and I'm much more confident doing the same thing in return.'

In order to be rude effectively, and in order to get away with it, you must appear confident. Simon's direct approach always works. He doesn't hold anything back. There is never any advance warning of what he's about to deliver and rarely any apology afterwards. This is a clear sign that he has confidence and belief in what he says. Similarly, if you, too, say it and mean it, there will be little room for a comeback from your victim.

'You're not ABBA; you're Flabba!'

This quote, directed at forty-seven-year-old twins Maura and Sally on *The X Factor*, reveals Simon at his most confident and effective. Predictably, the pair didn't look or sound remotely like Abba, and Simon's comment was spot on, but only he would have dared to have used the word 'Flabba'. He had the confidence to say what every viewer was thinking: that Abba were never fat, and that they could sing, too!

WIT

The Abba quote above also illustrates the importance of wit in the SSR. Indeed, the ability to be quick-witted is essential for anyone hoping to pursue Simon-style rudeness. Using a one-line rude comment like this can be the safest and most effective in the early days of learning to be rude. The trick is to keep it simple.

TIMING

The first rule of comedy is, of course, timing, and a sense of good timing is of the utmost importance in the art of being rude. You'll never get away with being rude if you can't time the impact and delivery of your put-down. Here's a selection of some of Simon's brilliantly timed attacks.

On *Pop Idol* when Pete Waterman accused Simon of judging people on their looks: 'If this competition was all about looks, you wouldn't have made it onto the panel!'

To Fiona Rae Griffiths on *The X Factor*: 'You look like Vicky Pollard and your friend looks like a stretched version of her.'

To Paul Holt, who had just finished singing 'End of My World': 'It's the end of your singing career, that's for sure.'

BODY LANGUAGE

You might have only ever seen Simon sitting behind the judging panel, but I can assure you that he knows all about the importance of body language. His walk is quick and steady, and when he enters a room he always smiles or laughs. He is notorious for getting the first word or comment in as quickly as possible. It's a fast, hard, full-frontal verbal assault, leaving no time for the victim to respond. To a man, he will deliver the put-down while shaking hands; to a woman he will do so while kissing her. This is the classic Simon approach, in which he demonstrates the first four key factors – self-confidence, wit, timing and body language – in one swift execution. Ouch!

One trick for those aspiring to Simon-like levels of rudeness is to watch his facial expressions. The way he raises his eyes to the roof when he's suffering yet another awful rendition of 'Flying Without Wings'. The hands on the head. The head on the desk;

the head on the floor; the legs in the air; The purposeful stare into the distance that means a rude comment is about to follow.

Learning how to use body language to your advantage will help enormously when being rude. Try staring purposefully over someone's shoulder or scratching yourself when someone is talking to you. Constantly asking someone to repeat themselves can also be terribly irritating and rude.

VOCABULARY

In the first part of this book I highlighted Simon's use of language and gave some examples of the kinds of words he uses to engineer the put-down or rude comment. Words like *appalling*, *terrible*, *dreadful*, *horrendous*, *hideous*, *ghastly* and *abysmal* are all used on a regular basis. Why? Because they can be applied as hard-hitting, one-word judgements, or in a sentence. For instance:

'I could only describe your voice as ghastly.'

'I think you're amazing. Amazingly dreadful.'

'You sang like some hideous singer on a cruise ship. Halfway through, I imagined the ship sinking.'

The words that you use in your put-down will make all the difference between a good put-down and a dreadful one. Look what happens when the wording of one of these comments is changed ever so slightly:

'I could only describe your voice as not very nice.'

I can't imagine Simon delivering that line on primetime TV! However, it clearly demonstrates the power and importance of choosing the correct wording for your put-down.

TONE OF VOICE

The importance of tone plays a huge part in communicating insults effectively. The voice is a weapon, and it should be used as such. However, those of you who are unfortunate enough to have a thin, high or weedy voice might experience problems early on when delivering a rude comment or put-down. Don't panic; there are many fine exponents of rudeness who have high or effeminate voices, although these are normally women.

If you're a guy with a slightly effeminate voice, however, you're in good company. Among our most famous comedians with rather distinctive voices and brilliant rudeness are Kenneth Williams and Joe Pasquale. Williams, in particular, used his voice to great comic effect and could be incredibly rude and funny at the drop of a hat. Pasquale, on the other hand, just has a silly voice but it didn't stop him from winning *I'm A Celebrity Get Me Out Of Here!*

Some observers claim that Simon's voice is slightly camp. Perhaps it is, but the way he uses his voice when delivering his comments shows that he knows the importance of tone. His voice doesn't vary in pitch at all, whether he uses it to deliver a trademark put-down or on the odd occasion when he praises a contestant. Keeping your tone constant is critical; if you get over-excited prior to delivering an insult, the pitch of your voice will rise and this will lessen the impact of what you say. Your voice and tone are power, so stay in control.

SIMONISMS

To help you on your way along the road to rudeness, it might be useful to learn some of what I call 'Simonisms'. These are little Simon-like pointers that will help you get into the rude mood:

- **'If I'm being honest'** – Always tell the truth. This is one of Simon's greatest strengths. If you don't like someone's shirt, tell them. Remember: you might be doing them an enormous favour in the process.

- **'I think I come over as a bit smug and self-righteous at times, and I imagine that could be annoying'** – Remember to be self-deprecating as this will take people by surprise. They won't expect someone who is rude to have this ability. It can therefore lull your victim into a false sense of security.

- **'I don't care what people say about me'** – This is a classic Simonism and demonstrates once more the importance of being confident. If you want to be rude, you must be strong and resilient in order to repel any comebacks. Your potential victims will soon become aware of your rude reputation, and this will make your job easier.

SUMMARY

In taking this first step on the road to rudeness, you'll need to learn and memorise the five key components:

1. Self-confidence;
2. Wit;
3. Timing;
4. Body language;
5. Vocabulary and tone.

Try chanting these five words in front of the mirror. Some people find that having a picture of Simon close by can also be helpful and reassuring, empowering them to scale new heights of rudeness.

Remember, however, to follow this programme one day at a time. Don't try to become rude overnight because it just won't work. The fact is that following the path to rudeness will change forever the way you live your life. This is just your first step.

THE RUDIMENTS OF RUDENESS

'Part of the problem is Simon's personality; part of it's his English humour. You can say to someone in England, "Oh my God, you're fat. Get off the TV!" and people will die laughing. [In the US], people will be, like, "You know what? That wasn't really a nice thing to say."

Randy Jackson, *American Idol* judge

SOME people believe that Americans are the rudest people on the planet. I don't think so. In fact, I believe they are far more polite than people in the UK. Randy Jackson's quote above demonstrates clearly just how Americans view the Brits. And the Dawg is soooo polite!

People in Britain are able to get away with so much more on television and in the press than the Americans. However, the rise of political correctness is beginning to taint all aspects of British life. It's time to rise up and fight back, and there has never been a better time to learn how to be rude.

Simon has a very clear view of political correctness, and it has become something of a pet hate of his. 'If you allowed the government to make a talent show,' he notes, 'you can imagine what it would be like. It would be horrific. Nobody would be allowed to insult anybody. Everybody would be a winner. The whole thing would be a shambles.' So, while Americans might find it hard to be as rude as the Brits, the Brits have more incentive to be rude. Don't let political correctness get in the way. Rudeness rules!

BEING RUDE CAN IMPROVE YOUR HEALTH

Most psychologists agree that it's healthy to vent one's spleen rather than to bottle up feelings, so making rudeness part of a healthy keep-fit regime is a great idea. I envisage a time in the very near future where 'Keep Rude and Healthy' clubs will spring up all over the UK and become the latest health fad. Indeed, such an endeavour could be Simon's next big franchise opportunity.

My message here is that you should never be afraid to be rude. It's healthy, honest and good for you. Don't ever be afraid of insulting anyone – as long as you tell the truth. This lesson should be used as part of your daily regime. Try reciting this simple morning mantra in front of your bathroom mirror:

'I am confident.
I am rude.
I am honest.
I am rude.'

Then repeat six times before leaving the house each morning.

STICKING TO YOUR REGIME OF RUDENESS

Just like any self-help programme, it's essential to set out your daily plan of rudeness. Make a list of your objectives. For instance, how many people do you plan to insult each day? Who are they? Making a target list is a good idea here, although it might vary depending on the season. Christmas, for example, is a great time for family rudeness, while a summer holiday provides fantastic opportunities for insulting foreigners or tourists.

Your daily rude regime might look something like this:

7:30am   Perform morning mantra.

8am   Be rude about partner's clothes

before he/she leaves for job interview.

11:30am Insult boss.

1pm Go to pub and be rude to barman for serving tourists before you.

7pm Tell partner his/her new hairstyle is crap.

10pm Pay homage to God of Rudeness by watching repeats of *The X Factor*.

11pm Perform rude meditation.

★

Sticking to a daily rude regime is essential and will help you to learn discipline in order to transcend the first level of rudeness. Think rude thoughts constantly and feel the force of rudeness. Practise quietly in the privacy of your own bed. Do not allow others to disturb your rudeness. Follow these steps and rudeness will enter your life. Trust in your higher rude power.

'Sharon's like one of those fish at the bottom of the ocean
that don't do anything till you swim near them, and then
they bite you from nowhere.'

THE RULERS OF RUDENESS

'Simon Cowell's ego is so large it is the only man-made object that can be seen from space.'
The Los Angeles Times

THE COMING OF THE SIMONITES

Purists would never admit that anyone could be ruder than Simon, but whether we choose to believe it or not, we have to accept that there might have been rude people here before Cowell (BC). The true followers of Cowell believe there is only one God of Rudeness. To his millions of disciples, he is known as the Prince of the Put-down or the Satan of Sarcasm.

Just as there are many forms of religion, there will always be those who believe in other Gods of Rudeness. Shocking as this might seem, we have to acknowledge there may be other rude religions out there. Therefore, in this section of the book we'll be exploring these so-called lesser Gods of Rudeness. To some – particularly the Simonites – these lesser or mini Gods of Rudeness were put there for a purpose: to show the way and to prepare us for the Coming of Cowell.

Whatever your belief, I'll endeavour to demonstrate to you that these ancient lesser gods had a minor part to play in the grand scheme of rudeness. By using examples, I'll show you how you can develop your rudeness, select your victim and choose your rude spot.

THE FORMER GODS OF RUDENESS AND HOW THEY CAN HELP

The realms of both politics and the arts have boasted numerous practitioners who have mastered the art of rudeness. These people had two things in common with Simon Cowell: they shared the same mammoth ego and the same ready wit. This wit is the key to rudeness, for without wit you'll never be able to get away with being rude. Learning the art of rudeness requires the talent to amuse. To get you in the mood, here are some classic examples of rude wit.

(Note: After completing this section, why not try reading some of the quotes out loud in front of the mirror? Dressing up as the person who originally gave the quote can sometimes help you get in the rude mood.)

OSCAR WILDE

Wilde was the Queen of Rudeness with a legendary wit. His ability to dismiss

anyone he didn't like with a vicious one-liner would have made him the perfect choice for a judge on *The X Factor*. In his time he was head of the pack and just like Simon, he crossed the Atlantic in a bid to try to educate the American people in the art of rudeness. Here, he failed – he was no American Idol – but his talent to amuse is every rude student's dream. Here are a few of his most cutting remarks:

'I don't like compliments, and I don't see why a man should think he is pleasing a woman enormously when he says to her a whole heap of things that he doesn't mean.'

'Whenever people agree with me, I always feel I must be wrong.'

'My own business always bores me to death. I prefer other people's.'

'We have really everything in common with America nowadays except, of course, language.'

MARGARET THATCHER

The Iron Lady had that magical combination of strength, self-belief and witty rudeness. Self-confidence was her driving power. For many years, most people believed in her ability to rule and in her firm judgment. Her lethal sense of rudeness was legendary, particularly behind closed doors at number ten. She too would have been a formidable judge alongside Simon Cowell, providing the ultimate battle of the egos. Among her most humorous asides are the following:

'I don't know what I would do without Whitelaw. Everyone should have a Willy.'

'I don't mind how much my ministers talk, so long as they do what I say.'

'If you set out to be liked, you would be prepared to compromise on anything at any time and you would achieve nothing.'

'If you want to cut your own throat, don't come to me for a bandage.'

WC FIELDS

The brilliant humourist is claimed by many students of rudeness to have epitomised rude wit. With his massive vocabulary, masterly speaking skills and unique outlook, Fields was certainly articulate. Like Simon, he knew how to deliver the ultimate put-down. His main purpose seemed to be to break as many rules as possible and cause the maximum amount of trouble for everybody. (Does that remind you of anyone?)

Here are a few examples of his work:

'A woman drove me to drink and I didn't even have the decency to thank her.'

'Anyone who hates children and animals can't be all bad.'

'Women are like elephants. I like to look at them, but I wouldn't want to own one.'

Remember to practise all of the above quotes in front of a mirror.

'I'm getting hundreds of emails every week and I have been threatened by people wielding baseball bats. People want to kill me. I just can't imagine why...'

PUTTING RUDENESS INTO PRACTICE

'I love *The Office*. I am literally addicted to that show. I relate to the boss, David Brent. We are both rude and unpopular.'

Simon Cowell

WHEN is it the right time to be rude? I've already talked about timing being the first rule of comedy. Like comedy, rudeness is an exact science that can be learned. In truth, it's never the right time to be rude, but once you've learned the rules of rudeness, you're rude for life and people will come to expect it of you. Remember: in the beginning, you *will* be unpopular – have no doubt about that – so you'll need to learn to be resilient.

Simon Cowell was already being rude at four years of age, and by the time he first appeared on television his family and friends had endured nearly forty years of his rudeness. By the same token, Simon has had to learn to live with being extremely unpopular for forty years. So get used to it.

Once you've gained the reputation and status of being rude, you'll find that many of your friends and family spend enormous amounts of time doing their best to avoid you. Don't despair, though; like Simon, from whom thousands of wannabe singers regularly queue up just to receive a tongue-lashing, you too will never be short of willing victims.

Having mastered the art of rudeness, you will immediately become known as a rude person. Rudeness will become your accepted way of life, and there will be no going back. Therefore, the right time to be rude is always.

The moment you lower your level of rudeness, you will invite your victim to strike back, so it's important to maintain a high level of rudeness at all times. For example, if you've delivered a rude comment to a victim, don't stop there; deliver a second, and then a third. That's what they expect of you. The more you're rude to someone, the less chance they have of responding.

Now here's your second daily mantra for your rude regime.

'I must be rude at every opportunity.
I must never stop being rude.
I must be consistently rude.
I must strive to raise myself to a higher level of rudeness.
I enjoy being rude and accept that I am unpopular [think Simon here].'

HOW TO RECOGNISE YOUR TARGET

Your victims will comprise people from various areas of your life, including the following:

- Family;
- Friends;
- Lovers;
- Colleagues;
- General public;
- People in restaurants;
- People in pubs;
- People in shops.

Take the first grouping here: Unlike Simon, you might wish only to *practise* your rudeness on family members. This is your choice and it will, of course, depend on the type of family you have, as there will always be certain members who will deserve your rudeness, ie mothers-in-law and children.

One only has to read a newspaper to note that the level of bad manners and rudeness among school children is on the increase, and it really is encouraging to note that many families are enjoying passing on rude tips to their children from a very early age. Kids will pick up on the rudeness you use around the house and quickly pass on tips for being rude to their school friends, thus ensuring a network of rudeness develops in your neighbourhood. (Incidentally, when being rude to children, it's important to note that the younger the child, the more chance you have of making them cry. This is always extremely satisfying.)

Start by learning to be rude to partners. As a beginner, it's so much easier to practise your rudeness on a partner or loved one. There's nothing wrong with this method and many feel this is what loved ones are there for.

To begin with, why not try some simple one-liners? This is level-one rudeness. Here are a few examples with a mild dose of sarcasm:

- Just as partner or loved one is placing your dinner on the table in front of you, avoid eye contact and say, 'About time too.'

- When serving you a morning cup of tea in bed, again avoid eye contact and say firmly, 'You're late this morning. Perhaps you need to get up earlier.'

- As your female partner puts on her underwear, this time make eye contact and say, 'Have you ever considered breast enlargements?'

The above examples are clearly aimed at married or long-term couples, but the early days of a relationship can provide additional opportunities for rudeness. Young females who are broody, for example, can often be very irritating to their male partners. They become pushy and often require putting in their place. If you're a man in such a position, try suggesting these simple alternatives when asked whether or not you'd like to have children. Using a light, non-aggressive tone may be useful here:

- 'Why don't we get a terrapin? They make cuddly pets.'

- 'Wouldn't you rather have a puppy? You can buy lovely little coats for them.'

DUMPING YOUR PARTNER

As an early test of your command of rudeness, why not try out your skills by dumping your partner, particularly if you're fed up to the back teeth with him or her? There's no easy way of doing this, so adopting a rude stance is best. Ultimately, you'll be doing your partner a huge favour; he or she will learn something through hearing your honest reasons for ending the relationship and will know better next time.

Here are some useful rude ways to dump your lover:

Invite your previously beloved out to a nice dinner – fancy restaurant, smart suit and champagne on ice. At an appropriate moment, drop down on one knee and pull out the special 'YOU WERE DUMPED ON 9 DECEMBER 2005' ring you've had made. Never fails.

Have your soon-to-be-former lover arrested for stalking. Show the police photos of you together as evidence. Scream every time you see them from now on.

Make a long list of your partner's faults. Get it published; read it out on national television; have it written in skywriting.

Pretend you have a terminal illness. Fake your own death after a few years. Have someone else's body incinerated at the funeral. Make an appearance and tell your partner you were just trying to get away from their ugly, ugly face.

Note: If you feel that you're not ready to dump your partner rudely face to face, you can now do it over the Internet. Sites such as www.urdumped.co.uk provide a dumping certificate that you can fill out, stating the reasons why you're doing the deed before sending it as an email.

MORE ONE-LINERS FROM LEVEL ONE RUDENESS

Try these out in mantra-fashion in front of the mirror. You might wish to use them at random in various rude situations:

- 'Thank you. We're all refreshed and challenged by your unique point of view.'

- 'I don't know what your problem is, but I'll bet it's hard to pronounce.'

- 'I'm already visualising the tape over your mouth.'

- 'It's a thankless job, but I've got a lot of Karma to burn off.'

- 'How about never? Is that good for you?'

- 'You sound reasonable. Time to up my medication.'

- 'I like you. You remind me of me when I was young and stupid.'

- 'I'm not being rude – you're just insignificant.'

- 'I will always cherish the initial misconceptions I had about you.'

- 'Yes, I am an agent of Satan, but my duties are largely ceremonial.'

- 'I'm really easy to get along with once you learn to worship me.'

- 'I'll try being nicer if you'll try being smarter.'

MAKING A RUDENESS PLANNER

'I think I've always been vile in real life. If I'm not being rude to anybody, I'm not doing my job properly.'

Simon Cowell

EVERYONE knows somebody they want to be rude to, so once you've mastered the rules of rudeness, why not write a rude hit-list to help you focus on who you're going to be rude to and where?

There will always be situations when it's absolutely necessary to be rude, so enjoy these opportunities. The following essential examples might help you when making your list:

- Bar staff who serve only the opposite sex;

- Shop assistants who gossip to each other and refuse to make eye contact;

- Posh restaurants and hotels with dress codes;

- Check-in staff at airports;

- Traffic wardens who put tickets on your car while ignoring your entreaties;

- Squawking children in restaurants;

- Coffee shops that are one big non-smoking section.

Now let's take a look at how you can be rude in any one of these situations:

RESTAURANT RUDERY

Simonites will already be aware how much the God of Rudeness hates being patronised in restaurants. He once complained, 'I can't stand people who patronise you in restaurants because you don't order the right things. It doesn't matter if you prefer baked beans to caviar. Who gives a shit? If you're paying for something, you're entitled to enjoy whatever you want. I would rather be happy eating my bowl of chips than pretend to enjoy a boiled pigeon with lobster sauce.'

Snobbery is just one of the problems commonly encountered in restaurants, and rudeness is the perfect response. French restaurants are particularly good at snobbery, and indeed the French themselves can also be quite rude, so you'll need to ensure you maintain the upper hand in this type of situation. Make sure that you appear confident and hold your head up high. Try practising the following rude tips at home beforehand:

- **Rude Tip 1** – Immediately on entering a French restaurant, ask the waiter whether or not he or she speaks English. If the answer is yes, ask if the restaurant serves English food.

- **Rude Tip 2** – Inform the wine waiter that you prefer Italian or British wines to French.

- **Rude Tip 3** – Keep asking the waiter to repeat himself or herself.

ARE YOU BEING SERVED?

Shopping can provide a whole host of golden opportunities in which to practise rudeness. For a start, there's nothing worse than being ignored by shop assistants. The key to this situation is not to shout or make a scene but to use your skills in rudeness and wit. Simon is always polite and courteous to shop assistants and waiters (he once worked as a waiter, although not for long, unsurprisingly), but the moment anyone patronises him or keeps him waiting, the rude mist descends. Remember the five key components of rudeness:

1. Self-confidence;
2. Wit;
3. Timing;
4. Body language;
5. Vocabulary and tone of voice.

- **Rude Tip 1** – Locate a well-known fashion shop where the shop assistants are known to ignore customers because they're so busy chatting to each other. When you finally get their attention, smile and say, 'Have you considered suing your brains for non-support?'

- **Rude Tip 2** – Alternatively, see what kind of reaction saying the following produces: 'I bet your brain feels as good as new, seeing as how you've never used it.'

- **Rude Tip 3** – Better still, ask the shop assistant where he or she shops for clothes, and then laugh hysterically at the response.

Next, here are some additional rude remarks that you can use to suit any number of situations at home, while shopping or when dealing with your partner or children. Again, you're best off trying these out at home, in front of your mantra mirror, in order to give each one the right tone of voice and body language:

'I married your mother because I wanted children. Imagine my disappointment when you came along.'

'Any similarity between you and a human being is purely coincidental.'

'Anyone who told you to be yourself couldn't have given you worse advice.'

'Are your parents siblings?'

'Did your parents ever ask you to run away from home?'

'Don't you have a terribly empty feeling in your skull?'

'Do you still love nature, despite what it did to you?'

'Every girl has the right to be ugly, but you've abused the privilege.'

'I'd like to see things from your point of view, but I can't seem to get my head that far up my arse.'

★

'I bet your mother has a loud bark.'

★

'I don't know what makes you so stupid, but it really works.'

★

'I know you're nobody's fool, but maybe someone will adopt you.'

★

'I'll never forget the first time we met although I'll keep trying.'

★

'I'm sorry but you've obviously mistaken me for someone who gives a damn.'

★

'If you don't want to give people a bad name, you'll have your children illegitimately.'

★

'Even your best friend cheats on you and lies to you, and that's the best friend you can get.'

★

'Ordinarily people live and learn. You just live.'

★

'I reprimanded my brother for mimicking you. I told him not to act like a fool.'

'I hear that when your mother first saw you, she decided to leave you on the front steps of a police station while she turned herself in.'

'We can always tell when you are lying: your lips move.'

'No one can be as calculatingly rude as the British, which amazes Americans, who do not understand studied insult and can offer only abuse as a substitute.'

'Oh my God, look at you! Was anyone else hurt in the accident?'

'Who picks your clothes? Stevie Wonder?'

'When he comes into a room, the mice jump on chairs.'

'I don't want you to turn the other cheek – it's just as ugly.'

★

'Marry me and I'll never look at another horse.'

'Either he's dead or my watch has stopped.'

'I've had a perfectly wonderful evening, but this wasn't it.'

THE CULT OF RUDENESS

NOW that you've mastered the first steps of rudeness, you're free to go out into the world to spread the rude word.

It's important to be evangelical about rudeness. A true Simonite has a duty, having learned the art, to offer something back to the God of Rudeness. This can take many forms. Remember that Simon is paid handsomely to be rude. He has made millions from simply being rude and teaching others the art of rudeness. Simon has made the world a ruder place, and we must learn to respect this and never begrudge him his rude riches. Many Simonites choose to offer him gifts of money as a sign of thanks for and appreciation of his work. Such contributions, however, are by no means compulsory; more important is your continued contribution to the world of rudeness.

To Simon's disciples, his message is clear: go forth and multiply. For added protection on your journey of rude discovery, you should study the Ten Rude Commandments listed below. These should stay with you forever and serve as your bible of rudeness and the first word of all true Simonites. Keep them with you at all times, as they will protect you against the perils of all that is good, polite and politically correct in this world.

THE TEN RUDE COMMANDMENTS
1. Go forth and spread the rude word.
2. Teach your friends to be rude.
3. Learn to love your rudeness.
4. Find a rude place and pray to Simon daily.
5. Avoid quiet and polite people, for they will irritate you.

6. Rudeness is your one true strength.
7. Always be cynical and sarcastic to others.
8. Do not tip.
9. Smile when being rude.
10. Always vote for Simon's acts.

FEEL THE FORCE OF RUDENESS

As you travel the road to rudeness, you will surely encounter those who will attempt to steer you away from your goal. These people – known as *rude reformers* – feel that rudeness is bad and should be eradicated, and you must avoid them at all costs. Do not allow them into your lives. You must always be on your guard and be prepared to deal with their wily do-good ways. They will try to tempt you from the path of rudeness with promises of salvation. Theirs is a life of grisly goodness, full of false hope and embarrassing kindness. You will need all your strength to repel these rude reformers, but never be afraid to use the full force of rudeness.

Rude Reformers dedicate their whole lives to the following:

a) Being overly kind to people who don't deserve it;
b) Patronising people;
c) Not telling people the truth to their face;
d) Giving others false hope;
e) Wearing too much make-up;
f) Telling fat people they look thin;
g) Never having cosmetic surgery;
h) Telling people who clearly can't hold a tune that they can sing;
i) Being envious of people with more money than themselves;
j) Crying in public;
k) Wearing weird clothes.

You must first learn how to recognise these rude reformers. To help you, I've identified a list of active members from around the world who have been found guilty of at least one or all of the above crimes against rudeness:

- **Sharon Osbourne** – Guilty of a, b, d, e and i, but definitely not g.
- **Paula Abdul** – Guilty of a–k.
- **Louis Walsh** – Guilty of e and k.
- **Ryan Seacrest** – Guilty of e, k and i.
- **Nicky Chapman** – Guilty of a, b, c, d and i.
- **Pete Waterman** – Guilty of a, b, c, d, i and k.
- **Randy Jackson** – Guilty of a, b, c, d, i and j.
- **Neil 'Doctor' Fox** – Guilty of j and i.
- **Richard Parks** – Guilty of j, i and of trying to imitate Simon and failing spectacularly.

If you meet any of these people, please try not to laugh.

Finally, in order to ensure that you remain rude and happy for the rest of your life, you'll find learning the following 'Desideruda' lots of fun. You might find it easier to sing it to the tune of either 'Flying Without Wings' or

'Unchained Melody'. Have fun, and may your life remain rude forever.

DESIDERUDA (WITH APOLOGIES TO MAX EHRMANN)

Go rudely amid the noise and haste, and remember what fun there may be in rudeness.

As far as possible, without surrender, be on rude terms with all persons. Speak your truth rudely and clearly, and do not listen to others, even the dull and the ignorant. Do not have a story.

Avoid quiet and passive persons; they are vexations to the spirit.

Before you compare yourself with others, you must become vain and bitter, for always there will be lesser persons than yourself.

Enjoy your achievements as well as your rudeness.

Keep interested in your own career. Never be humble; it is a real possession in the changing fortunes of time. Exercise rudeness in your business affairs for the world is full of thick people, but let this not blind you to what true rudeness is.

Strive to make more money.

And fill the world with rich celebrities.

Be yourself.

Feign affection.

Be cynical about love for, in the face of all aridity and disenchantment, love is a pain in the arse.

Ignore the counsel of the years.

Do not surrender the things of youth. Nurture rude spirits to shield you from misfortune, but do not stress yourself with nice imaginings. Many beers are drunk alone.

Be always a rude disciple. Be hard and cruel to others.

You are a child of the rude universe, no less than the trees and celebs.
You have a right to be rude.
And whether or not it is clear to you, the universe is unfolding as it should.

Therefore be at peace with Simon, whatever you conceive Him to be.
And whatever your labours and aspirations, in the noisy confusion of life, keep rudeness in your soul.

With all its sham, drudgery and broken dreams, it is still a rude world.
Be nasty and never strive to be nice.